SECRET TACOMA

A Guide to the Weird, Wonderful, and Obscure

Chris Staudinger

REEDY PRESS

Reedy Press
PO Box 5131
St. Louis, MO 63139
reedypress.com

Library of Congress Control Number: 2025936465
ISBN: 9781681066172

Design by Jill Halpin

Unless otherwise indicated, all photos are courtesy of the author or in the public domain.

Printed in the United States of America
25 26 27 28 29 5 4 3 2

CONTENTS

Allen C. Mason

ACKNOWLEDGMENTS

There is so much to say about Tacoma, and this just barely scratches the surface, but I owe so much to this community. The years and years of research that it takes to become a local guide and author were built slowly and over *many* trips to the archives, the library, and the hidden alleys of Tacoma. The incredible historians in Tacoma have worked so hard to preserve what this city has and make it accessible to us all. Lauren Hoogkamer always encouraged me to keep sharing Tacoma's legacy and assisted me with neighborhood resources. Allison Campbell guided my efforts in research and was pivotal in helping me navigate the Washington State History Museum. Iconic historians like Michael Sullivan have developed so many public-facing resources like Tacoma History Live and History Link that have shed new light on the region for me. Julia Berg with the Foss Seaport would dive into any story and find an expert to help corroborate details. Journalists like Steve Dunkelberger recommended insights and leads and helped foster my journey though Tacoma. Local author Peggy Cleveland set me on this journey to actually write some of the knowledge down. I am deeply grateful to the research assistance and clue-finding efforts of librarians like Spencer Bowman at the Tacoma Public Library. I also must acknowledge the hard work of Tacoma at large. Whenever I found a dead end in my research, there was always a friendly local online willing to share what they remembered from the past. This book is the culmination of years of relationship building in Tacoma and leaning on this city to help me tell its story.

Tacoma

INTRODUCTION

The first thing people think of when you say Tacoma is the aroma. Historically not in a positive way. You ask most people who aren't from here what they know about the city, and they will cringe while they list off the worst adjectives they know. This isn't really a fair assessment of a place known as the City of Destiny. Tacoma is a port town nestled along Puget Sound with a commanding view of Mount Rainier. The aroma of Tacoma has come from a lot of different sources over the last 100 years, and some of them have been admittedly awful. We have had a paper mill, a smelter, and some wild low tides. Make no mistake, Tacoma is gritty, but you know what? It is awfully pretty, too.

Many people don't know that Tacoma is more than just a stop along Interstate 5. It's a global hub, the gateway to the Pacific Northwest. Tacoma has a resident mummy, a glass bridge, a hidden train tunnel, and a coffee pot–shaped bar. There are treasures untold for anyone with some curiosity and courage.

The city took its name from the mountain nearby. There are many Indigenous tribes in the region, and each of them has a name for the mountain we call Rainier. Tahoma, Takhoma, Tacoma, Ta-co-bet, Taqo'ma, and Tkobed are a few of them, but Tacoma is the name that stuck for this city. Tacoma began as the terminus for the northern route of the transcontinental railroad and boomed into a thriving city that was lovingly known as the city "where rails meet sails." This city has taken some knocks, but through every up and down Tacoma remains steadfastly Tacoma. It is a place that takes care of its own and has created innovations seen worldwide.

The City of Destiny deserves a champion, and my hope is that anyone who reads this will be armed with the trivia and knowledge to go out and celebrate the bold, the weird, and the truly unbelievable trials and achievements of this great city.

GODDESS OF COMMERCE

Why is there a statue to the goddess of commerce in Tacoma?

When Tacoma was selected to become the terminus for the Northern Pacific Railroad, the international port was suddenly the most important in the region. From lumber to grain it was commerce that kept the city alive and booming. So, in 1885, when Tacoma built a new chamber of commerce, they wanted something to represent the power of the economy and the hope for the future. The architect, August Darmer, added the goddess statue to the roof to welcome success and business for ages to come. The statue was modeled after August's wife, Sofia Darmer. The first goddess statue held an axe, a fishing pole, and a railroad spike to reflect the most important businesses in Tacoma at the time. However, she was lost when the building was demolished

TACOMA'S PATRON

WHAT: The patron goddess of Tacoma

WHERE: On the corner of S Baker St. and St. Helens Ave.

COST: Free

PRO TIP: Bring a small offering to leave for the goddess so she can bless your business and finances.

The goddess seems to love her time in Tacoma. The city has one of the largest ports in the US and provides nearly $3 billion in economic activity for the county.

in 1950 after the terrible earthquake in 1949. The salvage crew that demolished the building, led by a man named Walt McHugh, sold the statue for scrap. McHugh used that profit to buy celebratory whiskey for his crew. It may seem a cruel fate, but I think the *Goddess of Commerce* would have at least enjoyed that a profit was made off her effigy.

Tacoma without its goddess just wasn't the same, though, and in 2009 local artist Marilyn Mahoney was tapped to design a new goddess statue to better reflect the business of Tacoma today. She looks like titan of industry Thea Foss, with shipping cranes for earrings, and in her hands are a cargo ship and Tacoma's historic buildings. Her outfit is brought together with a band of salmon. Today she stands watch over the city and ushers in a new age of success and business.

GRAY SHIPS

What are those massive ships docked along the Tacoma waterfront?

Looming over the shoreline are two mysterious ships that, though they gleam with the shine of well-maintained vessels, often seem unused. These two ships are actually the front line of disaster readiness and are waiting like well-trained first

responders. The SS *Cape Island* and the SS *Cape Intrepid* are sister ships originally launched in 1976. They once served the US Navy but today work for the US Department of Transportation. In 1993 they were retired from the navy and reassigned to the Maritime Administration's Ready Reserve Force. They are two of the 63 Roll-on/Roll-off ships in the Sealift Program and are kept ready at all times along the Tacoma waterfront to respond to any disaster in the region within five days. If, for example, there is a hurricane, earthquake, or even a military operation that needs supplies, these two gargantuan ships will be ready and waiting to distribute what is needed. They are very rarely deployed, though, and remain consistent figures on the Tacoma shoreline. Being strategically located next to a major port, alongside a main train line, in the shelter and safety of Tacoma's Commencement Bay, affords them protection from the wild Pacific, and they are close to the major hub of Seattle, as well as the main routes to Alaska and California.

THE REGION'S DEFENDERS

WHAT: Disaster response ships guarding the region

WHERE: 611 N Schuster Pkwy.

COST: Free to look at from afar

PRO TIP: The best vantage point to view the ships is from Chinese Reconciliation Park, where you can get a killer view of the bright-orange free-fall lifeboats, which are designed to launch from the stern and to dive into the water before bobbing back to the surface.

The ships are always ready with a live-aboard crew of 10 and a cargo capacity of 149,088 square feet.

HIDDEN BATHHOUSE

Did you know that there is a bathhouse beneath downtown Tacoma?

When Tacoma began as a hardworking port town, a lot of lumberjacks, railroad workers, and sailors came to the city to spend time and money. Many of these men didn't have homes in the area and needed a place to wash up before going out into society. Even beyond that, Tacoma was a beacon of civilization, and people came to the "big city" to see motion pictures and buy supplies from the small provincial towns in the region. Some of the symbols of luxury and civilization were the bathhouses Tacoma had in abundance. Norwegian, Swedish, Turkish, and Japanese bathhouses and steam rooms were perfect locations to get cleaned up before strolling the streets. One of these establishments was part of the downtown scene for generations until the building on top of it got wrapped up in local crime. The Kentucky Liquor Co. was first used as a headquarters for local crime boss Peter Sandberg. After his collapse from the throne of vice in 1931, Vito Cuttone became the new name in crime, and his name was whispered in the same breath as the shadowy bathhouse below the old Kentucky Liquor Co. building. Stories of murder, abduction, and retribution circled in the city for years until in the 1960s the building that housed both the bathhouse and

BENEATH THE STREETS

WHAT: A former bathhouse turned into a rain cistern

WHERE: 1250 Pacific Ave.

COST: Free to imagine

PRO TIP: Grab dinner at the Old Spaghetti Factory and tell your family and friends what is below the floor while you eat next to one of Tacoma's old streetcars now installed inside the restaurant.

the Kentucky Liquor Co. was demolished to make way for a modern sidewalk system and shopping center. By the time the building was demolished, most people had forgotten about the bathhouse and it was sealed up underground and forgotten. That is until a new business accidentally found it while working below their new offices. When they did discover it, they decided to make use of the perfectly tiled bathhouse as a rain cistern. Today Pacific Plaza uses the bathhouse to store rainwater collected throughout the wet parts of the year to feed their rooftop garden during the dryer months.

Many of Tacoma's basement-level establishments were simply boarded up in the 1960s and are still below the sidewalk today.

FAWCETT'S FAUCET

A FORMER MAYOR'S GIFT

WHAT: A dry drinking fountain

WHERE: 801 A St.

COST: Free

PRO TIP: Plan to walk the charming park. Most of Firefighter's Park was added to a man-made platform designed specifically to cover the 705 Highway that was added later in Tacoma's history. It's one of the few parks in Washington on an elevated platform.

What is that strange stone structure by Firefighter's Park?

You may have been confused by the large stone structure that sits in Firefighter's Park in downtown Tacoma. There is nothing to signal what it is other than some shallow stone bowls attached to the edges and a simple stone carving that states, "Presented by A. Fawcett." One of Tacoma's most famous mayors, Angelo Fawcett took a trip to Long Beach, California, in 1908 and saw a large drinking fountain along the boardwalk. He loved it so much that when he returned to Tacoma he paid $1,000 of his own money to have a fountain made. It used to sit right outside the Bostwick Building, across from the Panatages Theater, but by 1909 the local business owners demanded it be moved. There was a large public outcry that the free drinking fountain was a blight on the eyes. Turns out that *only* Mayor Fawcett liked the faucet, and so the whole fountain was moved to the obscure section of Firefighter's Park. The plan was to take it

Angelo Fawcett loved to give. In the economic depression of 1893, he fed more than 2,000 children with 75 turkeys, 500 pounds of potatoes, and pies that he bought himself.

to Point Defiance Park later, but it ended up being too heavy and the decision was made to leave it where it is. It was never hooked back up to the water supply, and over the years the precious metal bits were stripped from it, leaving the odd stone column we have today. Currently you can see the fountain still downtown, but sadly it no longer works.

Photo courtesy of Tacoma Public Library

THE SPANISH CANNON IN WRIGHT PARK

What do Cuba and Tacoma have in common?

Sitting proudly along the edge of Wright Park is a magnificent bronze cannon that was cast in Spain in 1784. It was in fact the 1,362nd cannon cast at this foundry in Spain, according to the inscription on the weapon. The long journey to Tacoma was an interesting one. The cannon first left Spain and ended up as a defensive gun on a fortress called Morro Castle in Cuba. During the Spanish–American War in 1898, the cannon was captured as a trophy by US forces and brought to Washington, DC. There, Senator Addison G. Foster procured the cannon as a gift for Tacoma and had it delivered to the city.

Addison was a big supporter of Tacoma after he moved to the area in the 1880s to follow business interests in coal and timber. The cannon was officially fired only once when

Photo courtesy of Tacoma Public Library

the battleship USS *Iowa* came to Tacoma and fired a sunset salute in 1900. The Spanish cannon fired a shot in response. That's the official record, but it did fire one last time in 1963. Over the years, some teens tried their hands at launching potatoes from the Spanish gun. They were successful in firing a mixed shot of rocks and potatoes from it in 1963, so the parks department had the long barrel filled in to prevent further shenanigans. Today, the bronze cannon enjoys its retirement in the shade.

TACOMA'S FAVORITE TROPHY

WHAT: A magnificent Spanish cannon from the 18th century

WHERE: The southeast corner of Wright Park

COST: Free

PRO TIP: Don't try to fire it. Please.

Many early cannons like this one have details similar to bells. That's because many of the artisans who made cannons also cast bells since the skills are similar.

THE NYMPHS

Why are there two European statues watching over Wright Park?

Standing guard outside Wright Park are two joyful young maidens, or nymphs. While these nymphs are celebrating love, it was ironically a short and unhappy marriage that brought them to the city of Tacoma from Europe. One of Tacoma's most active boosters was a man named Clinton Ferry. He was known affectionately as "the Duke of Tacoma" and gave himself the title of Colonel. Clinton believed that Tacoma would succeed if it could become more like Europe. His plans included building parks, sidewalks, and centers for culture and art. Tacoma's first official city park became Ferry Park, located at 1400 South Sheridan Avenue and donated by Clinton Ferry in May 1883. As the saying goes, being wise and in love is difficult even for the gods. Clinton was an excellent example of this in that he didn't always make shrewd decisions when it came to the heart. He had just remarried in the 1870s to a woman named Cynthia Trafton. The couple were married for a few happy years before going on their honeymoon to Europe. While there, Clinton went to Paris in 1886 as a representative for Washington Territory for the upcoming 1889 Parisian Exposition. During a three-year period, he collected European art, coins, military memorabilia, and cultural artifacts. Then Clinton and Cynthia returned to France to collect as much European art as they could with the intention of decorating their home in Tacoma. While in Paris Clinton left Cynthia with her French tutor and went out to

---

The two Greek maidens are named *Annie and Fannie*. Fannie used to have her hand on her chin, but it was broken in the mid-1900s. When she was restored, the artist put her hand across her waist to make her stronger.

procure some more art. He returned a little early to their suite and had the shock of his life when he found out she was having an affair with her French tutor. Heartbroken, Clinton gave away all the art to the city of Tacoma and left his new bride in Europe. He even established the Ferry Museum, which later became the Washington State History Research Center across from Stadium High School. Bad news for the Ferry family but great news for the rest of us.

EUROPEAN STATUES

WHAT: Two Greek nymphs celebrating the love of the region

WHERE: The north entrance of Wright Park

COST: Free

PRO TIP: Be good to your loved ones.

Photos courtesy of Tacoma Public Library

WHAT: A collection of subterranean rooms and businesses long forgotten

WHERE: The main downtown section of Tacoma

COST: Depends on the business

PRO TIP: The Tacoma Public Library's digital archive has several photos of the underground spaces in the city.

TACOMA'S TUNNEL NETWORK

Is there an underground Tacoma?

Anyone who has ever walked the streets of Tacoma knows all too well that the city is built directly into a very steep hill. The city managers and planners figured the best way to secure the new metropolis would be to terrace the city up the hill like a series of steps. This has led to some interesting architectural features, like the uphill portion of the main city core being underground. When you look at Tacoma you'll notice that the uphill side of the first floor of most buildings is tucked into the hillside. To make it even more exciting, a lot of these subterranean sections are connected, leading to an amazing world of businesses, passages, and offices all under the sidewalk. Many of these underground passages have glass blocks installed in the sidewalk, which allows the sun to shine down into the passages below. The underground areas include a collection of jail cells, bathrooms, hidden passages, mortuaries, and smuggling corridors that have been used over

Photo courtesy of Tacoma Public Library

the years for anything from local police stations to housing crime groups. During the 1960s there was a dedicated effort to get rid of Tacoma's seedier elements, so many of the subterranean locations were bricked up and forgotten.

Though sealed up, they often weren't filled in, so during the revitalization efforts of the 1990s many businesses and buildings ended up discovering old bathhouses, fallout shelters, tunnels, and secret rooms that had long been forgotten.

One of the largest tunnels in Tacoma was a train tunnel that the Union Pacific abandoned when it kept flooding.

THE BIRTHPLACE OF NOIR

What fateful accident may have led to the hard-boiled detective novel?

Dashiell Hammett, a former Pinkerton detective turned novelist, is widely credited with writing the first great detective novel, *The Maltese Falcon*. Though a poor detective—his only case solved involved a missing Ferris wheel—he was a gifted storyteller. After contracting tuberculosis, Hammett was dismissed by the Pinkerton agency and found himself in Tacoma's tuberculosis recovery ward in 1920. There, he explored the city and nearly met his end one fateful night.

Still known as Sam Hammett at the time, he was walking home from a speakeasy when he heard a gunshot and briefly thought he'd been shot. He returned to his hotel and slept, only to wake the next morning to a shocking article: "Sam Hammett, shot dead in the street." In reality, the victim was Sam Hamblet, a man walking home after visiting his son's newsstand. A rookie cop searching for a burglar had called out to Hamblet, who fled, mistaking the officer for a mugger. The cop fired a warning shot, which ricocheted off the sidewalk and killed Hamblet. Hammett, hearing the shot, had mistakenly believed he was the target.

While Tacoma doesn't have any Maltese falcons, it does have a mated pair of peregrine falcons that nest on top of one of Tacoma's tallest buildings, the building that once inspired Hammett's "Flitcraft Parable."

Photo courtesy of Tacoma Public Library

The incident deeply unsettled Hammett, prompting him to adopt his middle name, Dashiell, and pursue a career as a novelist. His first novel included the "Flitcraft Parable," in which a Tacoma man narrowly escapes death when an I-beam falls near him, leading him to start a new life. This story, echoing Hammett's own brush with mortality, suggests a deeply personal connection to his work.

TACOMA'S DETECTIVE STORY

WHAT: The birth of the detective novel

WHERE: The alley behind Courthouse Square at 1102 A St.

COST: Free

PRO TIP: Stop in at the McCallum & Sons Whiskey Co. nearby to get the full Prohibition-era effect.

A BANK VAULT YOU CAN HANG OUT IN

Photo courtesy of Tacoma Public Library

AN OLD BANK VAULT

WHAT: A former bank vault turned into a swanky hangout

WHERE: The basement of the National Bank of Tacoma Building

COST: You need to be a resident of the building or a friend of a resident to get access.

PRO TIP: Make friends with the residents and see if they are willing to host your next 1920s-themed party.

Where is the most secure hangout in Tacoma?

The National Bank of Tacoma Building opened in 1925 and was already famous by the time the front doors swung wide to welcome the city's business elite. It was a modern building for Tacoma and very exciting at 17 stories tall. At the time, it was the second-tallest building in the Pacific Northwest. The interior had a wide selection of businesses leasing space; among them were Brotherhood Cooperative, National Bank, Tacoma Oriental Steamship Co., Blyth & Co., Personal Finance Co., Washington Minor Hospital, Tacoma Club,

When the National Bank of Tacoma Building was built, it was the first in Washington to be designed to withstand earthquakes.

Photo courtesy of Astor Apartments

American Savings & Loan Assoc., Tacoma Merchants Credit Union, Great Northern Realty Co., United Mutual Savings Bank, and Sterling Financial Corp. These banks were supposed to be the most secure in the region and had a giant vault installed in the basement, with a mechanical floor that would drop down to allow the vault door to swing open or closed.

The National Bank of Tacoma Building had its ups and downs, but by the early 2000s it looked like it might not make it. An investor purchased the whole structure and turned it into apartments. The bank vault was transformed into a lounge called the Lock and Key, where residents can now gather and relax. Once it was the most secure vault in Tacoma, and today it's a safe spot to invest your time.

THE SEYMOUR BOTANICAL CONSERVATORY

Did early Tacoma have one of the best collections of tropical plants on the West Coast?

One of the most iconic parts of Tacoma's Wright Park is the jewel box conservatory building that opened in 1908 thanks to the dedicated efforts of William W. Seymour. Aside from its eye-catching beauty, the building is rather famous for being one of only three Victorian-style conservatories on the West Coast. It has more than 3,500 panes of glass and is home to a wide variety of tropical plants. No matter what the season or the weather outside, it is always a balmy summer day inside. When the Seymour Conservatory opened, it was the first time that many Tacoma residents had ever seen a tropical plant. The collection of figs, ferns, and orchids today is interwoven with a small pond and a terrarium with a species of rainforest frogs inside a special viewing habitat. The frogs are a collection of poison dart frogs, quite exotic. One of the most secretive parts of the building is the living wall.

The park surrounding the conservatory is an arboretum with several examples of champion trees. (Champion trees are the largest of their species.)

Photo courtesy of Pexels, Josh Hild

In the far wing is a division with built-in pockets that houses over 1,200 plants of 30 different species. It appears as though it was grown from the ground up, not built.

Seymour wanted there to be a place that would allow for the beautification of Tacoma and to provide a refuge from the hard work and trials of life, a sanctuary where visitors could relax and enjoy the majesty of nature. The fact that this stunning piece of architecture has survived for more than 100 years is a testament to the public's love of that idea. Today you can explore the jewel box conservatory and experience the rich tropical air and verdant plants of the world no matter the season. It's a small paradise nestled in the heart of Tacoma.

THE JEWEL BOX CONSERVATORY

WHAT: A Victorian-style jewel box conservatory

WHERE: The east edge of Wright Park, 316 S G St.

COST: Free but donations are encouraged when you enter

PRO TIP: Go in the winter to enjoy a tropical getaway during the coldest and darkest months of the year.

THE WORLD'S TALLEST AND LONGEST BICYCLE BRIDGE

Was Tacoma once home to a bridge used only for bicycles?

As a matter of fact, it was. A large gulch used to span between the eastern part of Tacoma and the main downtown corridor. Many people who worked downtown lived in East Tacoma, and they wanted a quick way to get to work and to the various downtown stores every day. The solution was proposed by a bicycle club known as the Tacoma Wheelmen in 1896. They wanted to institute a bicycle license fee to pay for the creation of a regional wonder. The longest and highest bridge exclusively for bicycles was built across the gulch that now makes up Interstate 5. It was a marvel to see. Spanning the full length of the gulch that divided East Tacoma from main Tacoma, the bridge in its heyday was 440 feet long and 127 feet tall. As a trestle bridge, it was designed and built by the carpenters and engineers

A BRIDGE ONLY FOR BICYCLES

WHAT: Historic bike bridge

WHERE: Delin Street Bridge near St. Mary's (520 S 30th St.)

COST: Free

PRO TIP: Take your bike over the Delin Street Bridge to get a feel for what the former bridge would have been like.

Tacoma might not have the world's tallest bicycle bridge anymore, but it does still have several bicycle clubs.

who had helped bring the railroad to Tacoma just a few years earlier. They designed it to be 12 feet wide at the top to allow for the simultaneous passage of multiple cyclists in either direction. When it was built, it set the Wheelmen back $984.50, or approximately $38,000 in today's dollars. The majesty of the bridge didn't last, though. By the 1930s the bridge was dismantled, and eventually the Delin Street Bridge went in as a replacement, with its sturdy concrete construction.

Photo courtesy of Tacoma Public Library

THE WHISTLING WELL

THE NOISIEST WATER SHAFT

WHAT: The world's noisiest well, maybe a gateway to the underworld

WHERE: Corner of N 33rd St. and N Stevens St.

COST: Free

PRO TIP: The well has been filled in, but the legends remain.

Is there a gigantic cavern underneath the city of Tacoma?

In 1891, Henry Lobe was living in what is now Tacoma's North End, on the corner of 34th Street and Mason Avenue. Looking to provide water for his household, he dug a well that ended up being 150 feet deep before it hit the waterline. The well was in his backyard, and it produced consistent water for his household until an earthquake a few months later changed everything. There were no visible changes to the well, but it suddenly began to blow air and dirt up from the hole. To measure the air, Lobe put a steam whistle on top of the well. The air was strong enough to make the whistle blow all day and all night long. Lobe's sleep-deprived neighbors threatened him to make sure he took the whistle down.

For years the well would not only blow air out but also suck air into the hole, and it stopped producing water. The weather seemed to affect it. The local Tacoma meteorologist came out to investigate and, sure enough, the well's action could be predicted by watching if the barometer fell or rose. Atmospheric pressure

---

The well isn't the only place in Tacoma that supposedly opens to the underworld. Local legend says that if you look at the summit of Mount Rainier at sunrise on the winter solstice, you can look into the land of the dead.

was a factor to whether air was rushing in or out of the hole. The meteorologist speculated that while Henry was digging that deep he accidentally hit an underground cavern and that during the earthquake the cavern was jostled around in a way so that when the weather changed, the pressure difference caused air to rush into the cavern or out of it. The hole for the well was large enough for someone to be lowered down into it, but on the few attempts Lobe made he was blown out of the hole. The decision was made to collapse the well. The mystery of the whistling well was never solved.

Photo courtesy of newspapers.com, The Tacoma Daily Ledger

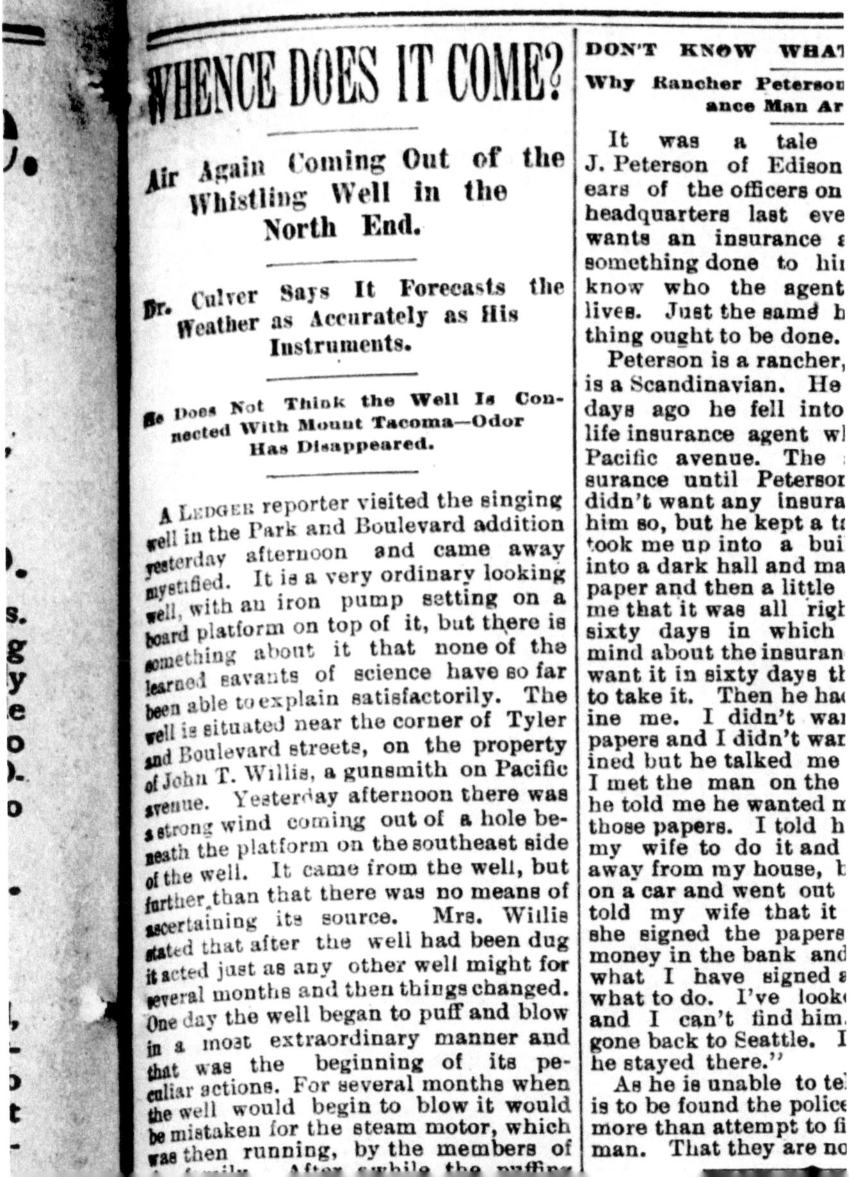

WHENCE DOES IT COME?

Air Again Coming Out of the Whistling Well in the North End.

Dr. Culver Says It Forecasts the Weather as Accurately as His Instruments.

He Does Not Think the Well Is Connected With Mount Tacoma—Odor Has Disappeared.

A LEDGER reporter visited the singing well in the Park and Boulevard addition yesterday afternoon and came away mystified. It is a very ordinary looking well, with an iron pump setting on a board platform on top of it, but there is something about it that none of the learned savants of science have so far been able to explain satisfactorily. The well is situated near the corner of Tyler and Boulevard streets, on the property of John T. Willis, a gunsmith on Pacific avenue. Yesterday afternoon there was a strong wind coming out of a hole beneath the platform on the southeast side of the well. It came from the well, but further than that there was no means of ascertaining its source. Mrs. Willis stated that after the well had been dug it acted just as any other well might for several months and then things changed. One day the well began to puff and blow in a most extraordinary manner and that was the beginning of its peculiar actions. For several months when the well would begin to blow it would be mistaken for the steam motor, which was then running, by the members of

DON'T KNOW WHA[T]

Why Rancher Peterso[n] ance Man Ar[...]

It was a tale J. Peterson of Edison ears of the officers on headquarters last eve wants an insurance something done to hi[m] know who the agent lives. Just the same b thing ought to be done.

Peterson is a rancher, is a Scandinavian. He days ago he fell into life insurance agent w[...] Pacific avenue. The surance until Peterso[n] didn't want any insura[nce] him so, but he kept a t[...] took me up into a bui[lding] into a dark hall and ma[...] paper and then a little me that it was all righ[t] sixty days in which mind about the insuran[ce] want it in sixty days t[...] to take it. Then he ha[d] ine me. I didn't wa[nt] papers and I didn't wa[nt] ined but he talked me I met the man on the he told me he wanted m[...] those papers. I told h[im] my wife to do it and away from my house, b[...] on a car and went out told my wife that it she signed the papers money in the bank and what I have signed a[...] what to do. I've look[ed] and I can't find him, gone back to Seattle. I he stayed there."

As he is unable to te[ll] is to be found the police more than attempt to fi[nd the] man. That they are no[...]

ST. LUKE'S MOVING CHURCH

Is Tacoma home to a moving church?

St. Luke's Memorial Episcopalian Church is an exact replica of a church in the English countryside. When the president of the Northern Pacific Railroad, Barstow Wright, came to Tacoma, he had St. Luke's built as a memorial to his late wife, Sue, and his daughter, Kate. Tacoma was on the map at the time as it had been selected to be the terminus for the Northern Pacific, and St. Luke's was a shining beacon of progress and beauty in a city that was on the rise. At the time it was built, St. Luke's was prominently placed in downtown Tacoma for all to see and visit. It was right at 602 Broadway, but you won't find it there today.

Sadly, the fortunes of Tacoma would rise and fall, and by the 1920s the congregation had all but abandoned the church, which was a little worse for wear. The community wanted to build more houses on the prime real estate downtown, so the church was selected for demolition in 1934. Tacomans heard this news and began to rally around the landmark. They saw it with new eyes, not as a blight on the skyline but as a historic treasure that needed to be preserved. The church couldn't stay where it was, though, so it was moved. A new plot was found in Tacoma's North End. In 1934, the community disassembled and numbered each stone and brick in the church one by one and carried them across town to the new location, where the church was lovingly reassembled piece by piece. The congregation took this opportunity to make the church a little longer, but the rest is the original design.

By 1947 the church had been reconsecrated and reassembled perfectly in its new home, where it continues to host services today.

THE TRAVELING CHURCH

WHAT: A Tacoma church that migrated almost four miles

WHERE: 3615 N Gove St.

COST: Free, if you want to go to church

PRO TIP: St. Luke's continues to host weekly services.

Tacoma has a history of moving some of its early buildings to new locations. The oldest house in Tacoma was also relocated to make room for new developments.

THE MOST ARTISTIC BRIDGE IN TOWN

WHAT: The Tacoma connection from downtown to the waterfront

WHERE: 1911 Pacific Ave.

COST: Free

PRO TIP: See how many cherubs you can find. The multiple Chihuly pieces feature a multitude of handblown cherubs hiding throughout the flowers and forms. Take the kids and make a game of it.

THE CHIHULY BRIDGE OF GLASS

Is there really a bridge of glass connecting Tacoma to the waterfront?

The name "glass bridge" might seem misleading when you arrive. The bridge itself is made of reinforced steel and concrete, but it has been elevated and bejeweled with 2,536 pieces of brilliant colorful glass. At 500 feet long, and soaring 70 feet in the air, it is the lifeline that ties downtown Tacoma to the water. In the early '90s there was a movement to clean up downtown. As the waterway was scrubbed and decontaminated, people wanted a way to connect with it and access it. A bridge across the dangerous train tracks was suggested, but no ordinary bridge would do. The Museum of Glass was being constructed on the far side of the tracks, and the bridge's architect began working with Tacoma native and internationally famous glass artist Dale Chihuly.

Chihuly designed the bridge to have three phases or stages. The first, as you cross from the city, is the Seaform Pavilion. In a suspended glass case, there are more than 2,364 pieces of art that represent sea life, Persian cones, and delicate aquatic flowers. Just a bit further down, two large towers of rough-hewn glass called the Crystal Towers frame Mount Rainier. They are at the center of the bridge and are designed to look like chunks of glacial ice. The towers feature 63 massive crystals of Polyvitro, a polyurethane that's extra durable.

The last phase of the bridge may be the most striking: the Venetian Wall. With 109 large glass art pieces, it dominates the skyline and invites pedestrians to stroll along the final stage of the glass bridge. Swirling between classic Venetian style and elegant Japanese floral arrangement, each glass addition delights the eye and whispers a line in the poem that is Tacoma.

There are several free-to-visit installations of Chihuly glass in downtown Tacoma. Within four blocks, you can see at least five Chihuly art installations.

TACOMA'S LIBERTY BELL

Why does Tacoma's US courthouse have a copy of the Liberty Bell?

During the 1950s, the US Treasury launched massive bond drives to raise funds, enlisting World War II heroes and national icons to travel the country by train, inspiring patriotism and encouraging citizens to invest. In the summer of 1950, the goal was to raise $650 million. As part of this effort, the Treasury commissioned a foundry in France to create exact replicas of Philadelphia's Liberty Bell. While sources disagree on the exact number—some say 55, others 53—Tacoma is confirmed to

have one of these replicas. These bells toured the nation on flatbed trucks and trains, serving as symbols of freedom and rallying points for bond sales.

When the replica bell arrived in Tacoma, it was displayed in front of the Bostwick Building and Pantages Theater at Broadway and 9th Street. Crowds gathered to hear speeches, enjoy music from Jason Lee Middle School's band, and admire the bell. This wasn't Tacoma's first encounter with a Liberty Bell. In 1915, the original Liberty Bell passed through the city on its way to the Panama–Pacific International Exposition in San Francisco. On July 14, 1915, more than 20,000 people flocked downtown to see the bell, which was paraded through the streets on a streetcar before continuing its journey.

After the 1950 bond drive, Tacoma's replica Liberty Bell was stored until the 1990s, when it was installed behind the federal courthouse in the newly repurposed Union Station. Once Tacoma's main train station, Union Station had fallen into disuse in the 1980s before being revitalized as a courthouse. The bell, a symbol of resilience and renewal, was brought out of storage to mark the building's transformation, echoing its role in inspiring civic pride decades earlier. Today, it stands as a testament to Tacoma's history and the enduring legacy of the Liberty Bell.

OUR OWN LIBERTY BELL

WHAT: A replica of the Liberty Bell

WHERE: Behind the federal courthouse located at 1717 Pacific Ave.

COST: Free

PRO TIP: You can ring the bell, but try not to annoy the security team too much.

Inside Union Station is equally dazzling. When the building was refurbished, it was filled with multiple Chihuly glass sculptures.

OLD ST. PETERS

What is Tacoma's oldest original building?

Photo courtesy of Tacoma Public Library

Nestled in Old Town Tacoma is a charming and unassuming little church that just happens to be the oldest original building in the city. In the early days, Tacoma was a wild port town that was mostly made up of unreputable boardinghouses and bars. The sailors would arrive from all over the world to do business with the booming lumber town and party along the main street. It was a dangerous and generally lawless place. That changed when Tacoma received a telegram proclaiming that it would become the terminus for the Northern Pacific Railroad. The town's business leaders proclaimed the need for a church after a visiting bishop named Benjamin Morris said that giving weekly services from inside the Chinese laundry building wouldn't work for a town that was up and coming.

The town leadership asked the people of Tacoma to come together and build the church. Enthusiasm for the project was dim until the 13 saloons in town said they would remain mostly closed until the church was completed. After that announcement, it took only seven days.

The church continues to house the original potbelly stove that was used to heat the interior.

Two fascinating parts of this church built in 1873 are unintended products of the hasty build. The walls ripple because the town didn't have time to cure the green lumber. The town also didn't expect to receive the 965-pound bell that was given to the church a year later. Two lumberjacks took the top off the old-growth cedar that was growing next door, and some sailors helped bring the bell aloft. When they counted the rings, the tree had over 300, making the bell tower the oldest in America. Sadly, the tree eventually fell due to rot and storms and was replaced much later with a steel pole. The church itself remains active here in Tacoma.

OLD TOWN'S FAMOUS CHURCH

WHAT: Tacoma's oldest original building

WHERE: 2910 N Starr St.

COST: Free, every Sunday

PRO TIP: Take note of the ivy outside. The invasive ivy was once so untended that it swallowed the church to the point where you couldn't see if from the street.

OLD CITY HALL'S JAIL CELLS

What lurks below the towering brick of Old City Hall?

Old City Hall is one of Tacoma's most beautiful buildings. It was finished in 1893 and had the big task of housing most of Tacoma's government in the basement: all the city offices, a library, and the police station. The city abandoned the building by 1959, and it has gone through several phases of reinvention since then, but through it all the jail cells below the street remain intact. Down below are several windowless jail cells that once housed Tacoma's most nefarious criminals.

The police operated from a headquarters in the basement of Old City Hall. Some of the cells were used for drunks, some for petty criminals, and a few were used to hold Tacoma's worst murderers. In the 1940s, one of the cells in the basement held a serial killer named Jake Bird. Jake was convicted in Tacoma for the murder of two women, but by the time he was executed he had confessed to the murders of 44 women across the country.

When city hall was abandoned during the 1950s the cells were left untouched until a restaurant and bar opened in the basement and used them for seating. You used to be able to get a table inside one of the old cells and listen to live music. Much of the graffiti that prisoners had left over the years was still on the walls when it was a restaurant in the 1970s.

A HAUNTED JAIL CELL

WHAT: An old jail block underground

WHERE: Beneath Old City Hall on the corner of Commerce and S 7th Sts.

COST: Dependent on business inside

PRO TIP: When you walk along Pacific Avenue you can see the old jail entrance in the alley on the north end of the building.

Later, the jail cells in the basement were completely empty, and several ghost stories started to circulate. One that still lingers is that Jake Bird's old cell door will sometimes slowly swing open at night. No one has ever stuck around to ask questions.

Old City Hall is currently being restored to its original splendor.

The police station was home to a dog named Sarsaparilla in 1905 who was used to "sweat" confessions out of prisoners.

SUB-SIDEWALK BATHROOM

Is there an underground toilet to nowhere?

When Tacoma was growing into a massive and modern city, the question came up: Where will everyone go to the bathroom? The answer came in the installation of comfort stations. These subterranean bathrooms began showing up along the main streets of Tacoma and were a good indication of how well-off the city was. However, as the years rolled on, many of them were just bricked up and then forgotten. That was the case with a particular men's restroom under the sidewalk by the Pantages Theater downtown. At some point, it was cut off from the rest of the city and left underground in darkness. When a theater employee heard a strange sound from the other side of a cinderblock wall in the basement prop room, the maintenance team got involved and made a hole in the wall big enough for a person to crawl through. On the other side, they found a fully functional bathroom with a urinal and toilet and several decades of grime and dust.

A RESTROOM FOR GHOSTS

WHAT: Tacoma's spookiest bathroom

WHERE: Below the sidewalk on the northern side of the Pantages Theater

COST: Free

PRO TIP: Make sure to go check out a show at the Pantages. It is the oldest of the Pantages theater chain that has continually operated as a theater.

Rumors that the old bathrooms were used as hidden storerooms during Prohibition have long been whispered in Tacoma.

No one knows for sure when it was bricked up, but today through a dark portal in the basement wall of Tacoma's grandest theater you can still hear the whisper of the 1920s across the marble floor.

TACOMA'S MOVING SIDEWALKS

Did Tacoma need mechanical sidewalks to handle the hills?

In the early 1960s, in an attempt to help people traverse the surprisingly steep hills of Tacoma, the city had four moving escalades installed downtown. These could help you get from Pacific Avenue to Commerce Street and from Commerce Street to Broadway, where the action was. The city demolished several buildings that they deemed part of the seedy side of town and used the new space to install the covered moving sidewalks. Each escalade was powered by an electric motor and fed out into the highly desirable areas of downtown. Not only did we

Photo courtesy of Tacoma Public Library

have a whole variety of iconic theaters along these blocks but also a great deal of shopping; the escalades encouraged people to spend and got them up the hills conveniently and safely. They were essentially covered tunnels so you would be protected from the rain.

Tacoma immediately set to billing itself as one of the most modern cities in the world now that it had electric sidewalks for your pleasure and comfort. The campaign worked. People were huge fans of the escalades down here in Tacoma, until eventually they fell into pretty significant disuse and disrepair. By the early 1980s, they had been boarded up due to a series of mechanical failures, vandalism, and people essentially using them as toilets. So the great escalades vanished from the city of Tacoma, but hopefully not from memory. Now you too know that we were once a shining modern city with moving sidewalks. The escalades were similar to what you might see at an airport today.

1960s MECHANICAL SIDEWALKS

WHAT: Lost moving sidewalks

WHERE: Near the fountains and ramps by the southern end of the Pantages Theater

COST: Free

PRO TIP: Explore the former shopping district and see the hidden mask art that is peppered throughout the theater district.

Tacoma gets steep very quickly. If you walked up 11th Street you could go from sea level to over 300 feet in about 13 blocks.

IVAN'S FACE PRINTS

Did a gorilla leave his face print on a window in Tacoma?

B&I mock-up of presidental visit.
Photo courtesy of Tacoma Public Library

B&I was established in 1946 by Earl Irwin and Leo Bradshaw. It began as an army surplus store after World War II. Eventually, Irwin took full ownership and transformed it into a Tacoma landmark. Known as the "Circus Store," B&I became famous for its eccentric mix of shops, restaurants, and unusual attractions, including Ivan the gorilla. Ivan, a lowland western gorilla captured in Africa, lived at B&I from 1967 to 1994 in a custom-built enclosure. His sister, Burma, died shortly after arrival, but Ivan became the store's star attraction, drawing crowds for decades. B&I also featured leopards and hosted publicity stunts, like appearances by the Cisco Kid, a popular TV character.

Earl Irwin was truly a marketing genius. In 1956, when President Eisenhower was planning to visit Tacoma, his team changed his route due to security concerns. So Irwin had a photo doctored to show the president driving past B&I with a line of

---

B&I is part of the attractions along South Tacoma Way. The main strip has historically had roadside curiosities, shopping, and automotive dealers. Many of them are still around today.

elephants holding signs—a testament to his creativity. After Irwin's death in 1973, his family continued running the store and caring for Ivan. However, as attitudes toward captive animals shifted, Ivan was relocated to the Woodland Park Zoo in Seattle in 1994 and later to the Atlanta Zoo, where he died in 2012. His legacy lives on through books, a stage production, a Disney movie, and the iconic statue at Tacoma's Point Defiance Zoo.

Today, B&I's gorilla enclosure remains mostly untouched, with Ivan's face prints still visible on the glass—a haunting reminder of its past. While B&I may seem out of place now, it was once Tacoma's premier shopping destination and remains a unique piece of local history. Plus, it's one of the few places where you can still trade old Nintendo games for cash. B&I's quirky charm and legacy continue to captivate those who visit.

Ivan at B&I. Photo courtesy of Tacoma Public Library

THE LEGACY OF IVAN THE GORILLA

WHAT: A circus-themed flea market with tons of history

WHERE: 8012 S Tacoma Way, Lakewood

COST: Depends on each shop, but admission is free.

PRO TIP: Check out the Disney movie about Ivan's life, *The One and Only Ivan*, before heading to the store.

BOB'S JAVA JIVE

Is there a bar that's shaped like a coffee pot?

One of the absolute coolest bars in all Tacoma is Bob's Java Jive. This concrete coffee pot got its start in the 1920s as a breakfast joint and then quickly turned into sort of a diner, drive-in, and dive place. Bob's first opened its doors in 1927 under the direction of a local veterinarian named Otis G. Button. Button wanted to open a breakfast location in Tacoma, and he loved the idea that his roadside attraction would be a giant coffee pot. In the 1950s Bob's really hit its stride by becoming a chaotic Polynesian-themed karaoke bar that billed itself as a music joint and dive bar.

The switch came when Bob Radonich and his wife, Lylabell, bought it and changed the name from The Coffee Pot Restaurant to Bob's Java Jive. Some of the artists from Tacoma's burgeoning music scene got their start at this little joint. Today, Bob's just percolates in local lore. Not only did they used to have two monkeys inside, but Neko Case also used to bartend, and most of the major acts of the Pacific Northwest have played here. It has a speakeasy bar behind the urinals, and Bob used to live in the apartment that is still on top of the establishment.

WHIMSY AND KARAOKE AT A DIVE BAR

WHAT: A coffee pot–shaped dive bar and karaoke joint

WHERE: 2102 S Tacoma Way

COST: Prices vary

PRO TIP: The first Friday in the month is often pirate-themed karaoke, where you dress like a pirate and sing whatever you like.

The Java Jive used to be home to two macaque monkeys, named Java and Jive. They lived inside, where patrons would feed them peanuts.

Photo courtesy of Wikimedia Commons

Keanu Reeves came and filmed several shots from *I Love You to Death* at Bob's and was even offered a chance to buy the Java Jive. Reeves wanted to accept the offer but with the condition that Bob's would be uprooted and taken to near his home on Maui. The owners wanted the Jive to stay in Tacoma, so they ultimately turned him down. Here in Tacoma, the Jive remains.

EARTHQUAKE STATUE

What is the tragedy associated with this North Tacoma statue?

One of Tacoma's saddest stories has been immortalized along North I Street with a bronze statue. On April 13, 1949, a major earthquake rocked the South Sound. The Olympia earthquake had a magnitude of 6.7. Kelcy Allen was a kindergartner at Lowell Elementary. When the earthquake began, he was inside the school as bricks and timbers began falling all around him. Allen fell down in the middle of the hallway and was sitting there when an 11-year-old hall patrol monitor named Marvin Klegman ran up to him and hoisted him to his feet. They ran together out of the building, Klegman throwing himself over Allen to protect him from the debris.

On February 28, 2001, 52 years later, the Nisqually quake rocked the region with a 6.8 magnitude earthquake. The event shook loose the memory that Allen had buried. He suddenly recalled a young boy pulling him up from the floor in the hallway and saying, "We gotta go!" Allen couldn't remember his name. He came back to Tacoma to do some research and uncovered a newspaper article from that day. He saw his own name in black ink on the page and next to it was the name of his savior. What Allen read next, though, nothing could have prepared him for. "Marvin Klegaman, 11, was killed on the Lowell school grounds." He was Tacoma's only casualty.

The artist who made the statue, Larry Anderson, also made some of Tacoma's other most iconic bronze sculptures, which appear throughout the city.

Suddenly all the memories came flooding back. Klegman had thrown himself on top of Allen to protect him and saved his life but lost his own.

Allen wanted to make sure Klegman was remembered. Civic activist Babe Lehrer read Allen's story and worked to get the funding for the statue outside Lowell. The statue, erected near the newly rebuilt Lowell Elementary, remembers Klegman's heroism.

A TRIBUTE TO A LOCAL HERO

WHAT: A statue to honor a young hero

WHERE: On the corner of N I St. and N 12th St.

COST: Free

PRO TIP: Just a couple blocks from the memorial statue is a plaque commemorating the home that Bing Crosby lived in for a few years before moving to Spokane. You can find it at 1112 N J St.

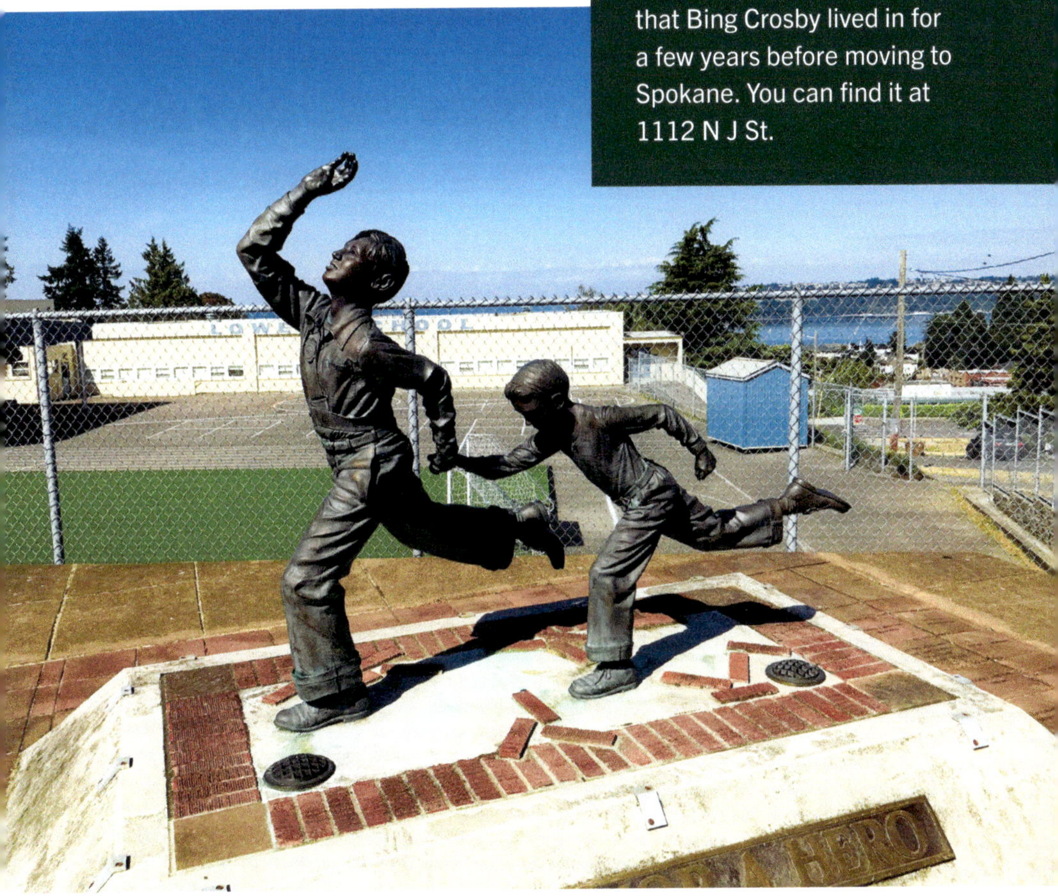

FOSS SEAPORT

Is this maritime museum the last section of America's longest warehouse?

Tacoma's identity has always been tied to its waterfront, earning it the nickname "the city where rails meet sails." In its early days, the port and train yards were closely intertwined, with trains often stopping just 15 feet from docked ships. To handle growing trade volumes, the city and Northern Pacific Railroad built a massive waterfront warehouse in 1900, part of which still stands today as the Foss Waterway Seaport, Tacoma's premier maritime museum. At its peak, the Balfour Dock Building stretched from Thea Foss Park to the 11th Street Bridge, forming the world's longest grain warehouse.

Constructed by railroad carpenters, the building's truss roof resembles the railroad bridges of the early 20th century. Trains pulled up alongside the warehouse, while ships docked on the opposite side, enabling seamless transfer of grain from rail to ship for international trade. It allegedly served as a gateway for smugglers too. There were often rumors of opium and illegal Canadian liquor being transported through the floor into a secret compartment inside. When the building was remodeled the crew found a secret hatch that was hidden below the carpet, a clue to what used to happen inside.

The Foss Waterway Seaport occupies the last surviving section of the once-mile-long warehouse. Fires destroyed other sections over the years, but brick firewalls effectively

---

The seaport and the adjacent waterway were renamed Foss in honor of Norwegian immigrant and pillar of the community Thea Foss, who founded one of the largest maritime companies in the US while she was living along the waterfront in the late 1800s.

Inset: Interior of Foss as largest wheat warehouse in the world, circa 1903. Photo courtesy of Tacoma Public Library. Bottom: Smuggling hatch. Photo courtesy of Jan Adams.

THE LOCAL MARITIME MUSEUM

WHAT: A maritime museum in a 100-plus-year-old waterfront warehouse

WHERE: 705 Dock St.

COST: Free

PRO TIP: For the full maritime experience, try to visit on a day when one of the tall ships, like the *Lady Washington*, is docked at the seaport and score a tour onboard.

contained the damage. When the seaport opened, it replaced one firewall with a glass wall, offering visitors a glimpse into Tacoma's maritime history. Inside, exhibits celebrate the city's legacy, from the Puyallup Tribe's heritage to the transformative impact of railroads. A collection of handmade boats, touch tanks, and interactive displays bring the region's nautical past to life.

As a museum, event space, educational facility, and working dock, the Foss Waterway Seaport remains Tacoma's vital link to its maritime roots, preserving the city's connection to the sea for future generations.

HIDDEN MURAL

A FORGOTTEN PAINTING

WHAT: A forgotten mural of Tacoma's women

WHERE: Between the buildings at 7 N Tacoma Ave. and 1 N Tacoma Ave.

COST: Free

PRO TIP: If you go to the alley behind 7 N Tacoma Ave., you can still see the mural if you look at the right angle.

Is there a hidden mural in the Stadium District?

In 2002, a building with an important mural was constructed in Tacoma's Stadium District on the corner lot of Tacoma Avenue and Division Street. The mural was painted by local artist Mary Mann in 1995 and told the story of the women who helped shape the city of Tacoma. From left to right the women were a member of the Puyallup tribe, a suffragette, a flapper, and a modern woman.

Photo courtesy of newspapers.com, Tacoma News Tribune

The women in the mural became pillars as they extended down the painting. This represented them being the pillars of the community.

Mann had wanted each woman to resemble a Greek goddess in some aspect. Behind them, the city of Tacoma unfurled from left to right as it moved from lumber camp to bustling industrial city. Fittingly enough, progress could not be stopped, and just seven years after the mural was finished, the corner lot was occupied by a multiuse building promising to bring more business and opportunity to the Stadium District. The catch was that it was going up three stories just eight inches away from the building that was proudly adorned with the new mural. The mural still sleeps on the side of the building, perfectly preserved and ultimately forgotten. The women that adorn it have vanished into the dark cracks of progress. Hundreds of people pass by it every day and have no idea of the story that sits between the two buildings.

Tacoma has a long tradition of adding murals to empty spaces to help tell the story of the city. The city keeps an interactive map to help you locate all of them.

CHUTES AND LADDERS

Have you ever wanted to play real-life Chutes and Ladders?

Well, now you can. Along the waterfront in Point Defiance Park is a 50-foot-tall series of slides that lets you experience the ups and downs of life. The six slides run parallel to a series of six sets of stairs. From the top, you can take the slide or stairs down or alternate between them. The whole installation was part of the waterfront improvement project that broght us Dune Peninsula at Point Defiance Park. The dune sits on top of a multigenerational molten-lead slag heap. The nearby ASARCO smelting company had been producing refined copper on the site for almost 100 years. A by-product of that was a slurry of molten lead and arsenic, which was dumped into the nearby bay to create a breakwater for the local yacht club.

Over the years, as the environmental protection procedures improved, and the smelter's fortunes dwindled, the conversation about what to do with the slag heap changed. The park was a brilliant plan to remediate the site and turn it into something safe and functional. It was named after locally raised author Frank Herbert, who wrote

STAIRS AND SLIDES

WHAT: A series of slides and steps to get you up or let you get down

WHERE: The boat launch at Point Defiance Park

COST: Free

PRO TIP: Take the family and some dice to make it a game, or set aside the time to cross the bridge and explore the rest of Point Defiance Park.

The bridge at the top of the slides has become one of the most romantic places in Tacoma to propose.

the Dune series. His novels about geopolitical ramifications and the ethics of environmental damages were directly inspired by his time growing up near the ASARCO site. Today the chutes and ladders site overlooks the old ASARCO smelting operation foundation and reminds us of the ups and downs a city goes through as it tries to move forward.

TRASHASAURUS REX

Is Tacoma's only dinosaur made of motorcycle parts?

Back around 2015, a local artist made a T-Rex out of scrap parts and rigged it up in his backyard. Some years later, he managed to sell it to a local company that set it up on Jefferson Street. There was a lot of mystery about the artist, but legend says he was a student at University of Washington with a passion for welding and a flair for the dramatic. When the T-Rex first made

its debut, it was in a yard of a college house near the University of Puget Sound on Alder Street. The amazing part of the T-Rex was that it had a makeshift pump inside that allowed it to breathe fire on command.

Alas, all good pyrotechnics must come to an end. A part of the sale stipulated that the fire breath had to be disconnected to prevent any unknowing pedestrians who happened by from catching fire. The *Trashasaurus* moved to its current home on the corner of Jefferson Avenue and South 23rd Street. Washington State has found only one dinosaur fossil, the Suciasaurus rex; but you know what? It didn't even breathe fire. I would like to suggest the *Trashasaurus Rex* as a solid alternative to the state dinosaur.

ART THAT'S FIGHTING EXTINCTION

WHAT: Tacoma's last dinosaur, made of motorcycle parts

WHERE: The corner of Jefferson Ave. and S 23rd St.

COST: Free

PRO TIP: You can still see the spot where the fire came out with a fine mist of gasoline.

The only dinosaur fossil discovered in Washington was made the official state dinosaur by students from local Elmhurst Elementary near Tacoma. They were researching how a bill becomes a law and made the push to get it named.

THE BREWERY LAMP POST

What is that mysterious post in Tacoma?

If you've ever driven or walked around on 25th Street and seen that mysterious concrete pillar, you too may have wondered what you were seeing. The good news is, we have the answer for you. All those brick structures out there used to be part of the Pacific Brewing and Malting Company, where they produced much of Tacoma's beer. During Prohibition, many of those buildings started making soap. One of them also began producing large blocks of ice. In a time before refrigerators, you often had to buy blocks of ice and put them in an insulated box, where you would keep your food. These were called iceboxes.

The pillar, however, is part of one of the last buildings added to the

What Goes on Here? – No. 10

Photo courtesy of Tacoma Public Library

QUAINT LAMP POST AT 25TH AND HOLGATE

Shades of Tacoma's Gaslight Era

By ERNA BENCE

From a few blocks off sounded the blare of a brass band.

Throngs were pouring into the city by survey, spring wagon, bicycle and horseless carriage. It was parade day in Tacoma, around the turn of the century.

With a thunderous rumble, massive barrel-laden trucks rolled over the bricks of the courtyard and out under the ornate arched entrance of the Pacific Brewing and Malting Co., at what is now South 25th and Holgate Streets.

Harness of high-stepping, satin-coated draft horses gleamed in the sunshine as they clop-clopped in triple hitch to join the procession. Plumes waved, vying their color with scarlet coats of the men on the box.

Lamp Post Remains

Today, all that's left of the glamor and Victorian grandeur is a forgotten lamp post.

Lonely, its twin long vanished, its graceful arch long demolished, it waits wistful and broken beside a row of garages at South 25th and Holgate Streets, midway between Jefferson and Pacific Avenues.

THE MYSTERIOUS MONOLITH

WHAT: An old gas lamp that used to mark the edge of the brewery district

WHERE: On the corner of S 25th St. and S Holgate St.

COST: Free

PRO TIP: Go during the holidays and see the former Tacoma Ice Co. turned into Tacoma Self Storage. They will turn off the "S" on their sign so it reads as Tacoma Elf Storage.

brewery complex. It was a gas lamp for the wagon shop. The local brewery would deliver its beer by horse-drawn carriage, and to light the entrance they had two large gas lamps placed on either side of the gate. The lamps were first installed in 1913, but over the years they fell into disuse and eventually were turned off as the brewery closed.

There was a large metal fixture on top of the gas lamp originally, and it was most likely removed to be used for scrap steel. While the gas lamps may be shut off today, the historic community here had two similar posts made to hold the gate for Tacoma Self Storage just down the street.

Much of Tacoma's historic brewery district kept its original buildings, and today it houses a variety of local businesses.

TACOMA'S MISSING CHINATOWN

Why is Tacoma the largest city on the West Coast without a historic Chinatown district?

Tacoma is the only major West Coast city without a Chinatown, but it wasn't always this way. In the late 19th century, a thriving Chinatown existed along the waterfront between Old Town and New Tacoma. However, anti-Chinese sentiment reached a boiling point in the 1870s, culminating in a tragic event on November 3, 1885. Led by Mayor Jacob Weisbach, a mob of armed townspeople descended on Tacoma's Chinatown, forcibly evicting around 200 Chinese residents—men, women, and children—at gunpoint. They were marched eight miles to a train station in what is now Lakewood. While some wealthier individuals could afford train fare, others waited in freezing rain for a freight train, with several dying from exposure. Those who tried to bring belongings were beaten and left in the streets.

THE TRAGEDY OF TACOMA'S PAST

WHAT: A park acknowledging one of the worst times in Tacoma's history

WHERE: 1741 N Schuster Pkwy.

COST: Free

PRO TIP: Every year the park hosts a celebration for the Lunar New Year and several events to help advocate for peace and anti-racist programs in Tacoma and beyond.

The structure in Chinese Reconciliation Park is called a *ting* and was constructed in Tacoma's sister city, Fuzhou, before being brought to Tacoma.

After the expulsion, the mob returned to Tacoma and burned Chinatown to the ground, erasing it entirely. In a cruel twist, some blamed Chinese resident Ah Chung Charley for the arson, leading to his arrest, though he was later acquitted. This marked the start of a decades-long campaign to exclude Chinese people from Tacoma. Despite 27 men being indicted for their roles, none were punished, and some even became prominent city leaders.

For more than a century, the event was largely ignored until 1991, when citizens, led by David Murdock, advocated for reconciliation. In 2011, Chinese Reconciliation Park opened along the waterfront, honoring the contributions of early Chinese residents and acknowledging the injustice they endured. The park features a history exhibit and serves as a poignant reminder of the past and a call to do better. Today, it stands as a place of reflection and education, ensuring this dark chapter of Tacoma's history is never forgotten.

AN OLD SCIENTIFIC ZOO ON THE ROOF

Was a downtown menagerie in danger of being overrun by guinea pigs?

Photo courtesy of Tacoma Public Library

RABBITS AND PIGS LIVE HIGH

Regular Menagerie Atop Washington Bldg.

Many Animals Living High Life in Interest of Science; Used for Serums, Experimental Work

Photo courtesy of newspapers.com, The Tacoma Daily Ledger

In the 1920s, Tacoma was at the forefront of using scientific methods to combat disease and solve crimes. The city had been pushed toward modern approaches by famed chemist and crime scene forensic scientist Oscar Heinrich, better known as the American Sherlock Holmes. One of the many advancements Tacoma made was using animals for testing. On top of the Washington Building on Pacific Avenue and 11th Street was a laboratory that raised giant Flemish rabbits, rats, mice, and guinea pigs. Each species had a role to play. One of the strongest contributors was the Flemish rabbits. These gentle giants were used to test blood at crime scenes. The process is called a precipitin test. Scientists could differentiate between human blood and animal blood by injecting a rabbit with blood collected from a crime scene. The rabbits would produce detectable antibodies if the blood injected into them was from a human, but they wouldn't produce these antibodies if it was animal blood.

The mice and the guinea pigs were used to help develop serums to combat diseases like typhoid and tuberculosis. This was a time when there weren't the same chemical tests that we have today. By injecting these viruses into the animals the doctors would then dissect the animals and see what effects the virus had on the organs to determine what parts of their human patients were most at risk.

SKY-HIGH ZOO

WHAT: A former scientific zoo that solved crimes and cured diseases

WHERE: 1019 Pacific Ave.

COST: Free

PRO TIP: The zoo is gone today, but eagle-eyed observers can see the pair of peregrine falcons that now patrol the skies by the old zoo.

The local newspaper noted that each of the rodents was accomplished at helping to identify disease and to help render a prognosis for many of the patients in Tacoma. In fact, the biggest problem the zoo had was that the guinea pigs had babies so quickly that the lab was often on the brink of being overrun. Over the years, the science got better and, luckily, the need to use rabbits as pregnancy tests has stopped.

In the 1920s, Tacoma had one of the largest tuberculosis hospitals in the nation.

ZANETTA AND THE TURNIP

TACOMA'S ONCE TALLEST BUILDING

WHAT: Once the tallest building in Washington

WHERE: 1119 Pacific Ave.

COST: Free

PRO TIP: Take some root vegetables and see if you and your friends can catch them.

Was catching root vegetables the most exciting entertainment in Tacoma?

The National Realty Building in downtown Tacoma constructed in 1910 was once the tallest building on the West Coast. Of course, Smith Tower up in Seattle surpassed it in 1914, but that's not what's interesting here. To celebrate this 16-story, 230-foot building being the tallest on the West Coast, the City of Tacoma decided to have a celebration. The main act was a circus performer named Zanetta. This wandering performer had a special skill. He would put a fork in his mouth and catch a turnip thrown from any height on the tines of the fork.

Zanetta was informed that he had three opportunities to catch a turnip thrown from the top of this tower. If he got it in the first try, he would get 100 bucks; second try, 50 bucks; if it took him three or more, he wouldn't get anything.

In 1910 the National Realty Building was considered a skyscraper because it was more than 10 stories high. Today it is widely believed that a skyscraper has to be more than 330 feet, so the National Realty Building wouldn't count anymore.

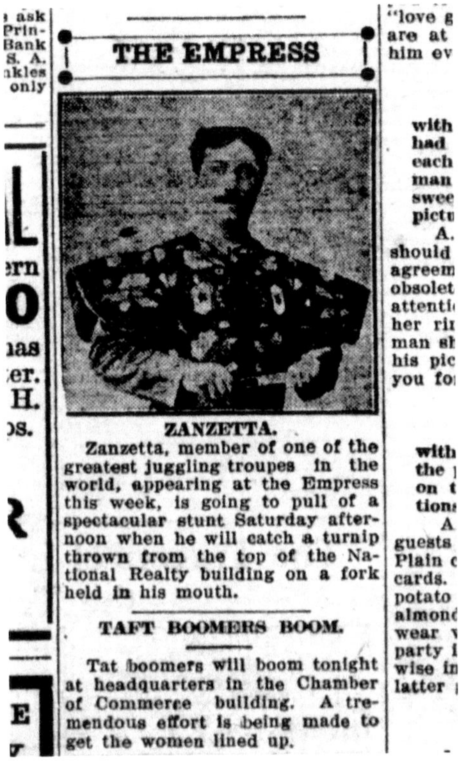

THE EMPRESS

ZANZETTA.

Zanzetta, member of one of the greatest juggling troupes in the world, appearing at the Empress this week, is going to pull of a spectacular stunt Saturday afternoon when he will catch a turnip thrown from the top of the National Realty building on a fork held in his mouth.

TAFT BOOMERS BOOM.

Tat boomers will boom tonight at headquarters in the Chamber of Commerce building. A tremendous effort is being made to get the women lined up.

Left: Photo courtesy of newspapers.com, The Tacoma Times
Right: Photo courtesy of Tacoma Public Library

On that fateful day, the citizens of Tacoma got together and watched Zanetta catch a turnip dropped from 233 feet up on the third try, thus getting no fame nor money. He did, however, narrowly avoid being knocked into the next year. And while, sure, he got no money out of the whole thing, it's still really impressive to catch a turnip thrown from over 230 feet on the tines of a fork that you're holding in your mouth. So it's just a reminder to never turn up your nose at a good act.

TELEPHONE MUSEUM

What is the empty telecommunications building hiding inside?

Did you know that Tacoma has its very own telephone museum? It is a testament to the long history of telecommunications in the region. It's only open on Thursdays from 8 a.m. to noon, but it is a wonderful look at the way phones have changed the course of Tacoma. The Tacoma Telephone Pioneer Museum is on the ground floor of the AT&T building, which was originally constructed in 1931 and housed the Pacific Telephone and Telegram Company until they eliminated their operator program in 1993. The telephone museum today is staffed by volunteers who have all worked in the telephone industry from the '60s onward. One of the things that is so cool about it is that the phones still work. So when you go in there, one of the women who used to work as an operator can actually walk you through the process of how you would deal with a call as an operator. For those with a mechanical mind, you can see the switching panels and the routing mechanism. One room is dedicated just to the physical phones themselves, and you can see the evolution from wall-mounted phones from the 1930s to the novelty phones of the 1990s.

FORGOTTEN PHONES

WHAT: A telecom building that houses the history of phones in Tacoma

WHERE: 757 Fawcett Ave.

COST: Fee for admission

PRO TIP: Ask if you can help work the operator board and get a firsthand experience of what taking a call in the 1930s would be like.

The building that holds the telephone museum still operates as a hub for AT&T.

Visitors can experience several amazing artifacts like a vintage telephone in which the mouthpiece was actually made of glass so that it could be removed and cleaned during the period of Spanish influenza. The building has served as a communications hub for the last 100-plus years and now affords a genuinely interesting and hands-on opportunity to go through telecommunications throughout Tacoma's history. If you're in Tacoma, give them a call.

POST OFFICE PEEPHOLES

Does Tacoma still have signs of America's oldest federal law enforcement agency?

The theft of mail became a federal crime in 1792, and new precautions had to be put into place to ensure that people's mail wouldn't go missing. The Postal Inspection Service is actually the oldest federal law enforcement agency in America. A large part of an inspector's job was to monitor postal employees and make sure they weren't stealing money or valuables from the post. However, what was the most efficient way to do that in the 1800s?

HIDDEN VIEWING PASSAGE FOR SECURITY

WHAT: Secret windows for watching former postal employees

WHERE: Along the upper wall inside 1102 A St.

COST: Free

PRO TIP: Court House Square has a whole variety of services and local businesses inside it today, so when you go to check out the observation windows consider staying for a coffee or dinner.

As it turns out, the answer was to construct several secret catwalks and corridors inside postal buildings. Most of the early post offices in America were built with a secret system of pathways inside and a mystery entrance on the exterior so that postal inspectors could enter the building and observe the postal workers completely unknown. This was part of the success of the program. Postal employees never knew if they were being watched or not and had to always assume that they were.

The federal building in Tacoma was built in 1908 and opened in 1910. It was constructed to house the federal customs house, post office, and courtrooms. To this day, it still houses a post office. If

Photo courtesy of Tacoma Public Library

you look up along the walls in the post office section, you can see small boxes with black glass in the middle. These are one-way windows that are attached to the secret corridors. Today the postal service doesn't use the secret corridors to watch their employees . . . or does it?

There are remnants of the federal building's old life all over. On the third floor, there is still a cell that was used for holding prisoners during court.

BLUE MOUSE

What is Tacoma's oldest continuously operating theater?

Top photo courtesy of Tacoma Public Library

The first Blue Mouse Theatre was built in Tacoma's prominent downtown theater district and opened in 1922, but that one was destroyed in the 1960s to make way for Tacoma's moving sidewalks. The second Blue Mouse Theatre was built in 1923 in the Proctor Neighborhood of Tacoma. The second theater, at 221 seats, may have been smaller in size, but its impact in the community has been enormous. The first film shown there was *The Green Goddess*. The theater was an instant success.

The Blue's Mouse's popularity soared, and in 1932 a local businessman named Will Conner purchased the building and renamed it to the Proctor Theater. Mr. Conner continued to run the

---

The blue neon lights in the shape of mice running along the marquee were designed by local sensation Dale Chihuly.

joint until the 1970s and renamed it the Bijou. By the 1980s the fate of the theater became unclear. With the ease of movie rentals and bigger chains moving in, the need for a small boutique theater didn't seem as pressing.

A local group of advocates banded together in 1993 and bought the theater, returning its original name, the Blue Mouse. They reopened the space as a community theater, and to this day it plays both blockbuster hits and local indie films. One of the great traditions of the Blue Mouse is the midnight showing of *The Rocky Horror Picture Show*. When the Blue Mouse Association reopened the theater, they restored it to its original grandeur and added some true Tacoma flair. The theater continues to be an icon for the region and simply refuses to quit.

A CHARMING HISTORIC THEATER

WHAT: One of the oldest continuously operating theaters in the country

WHERE: 2611 N Proctor St.

COST: Fee for admission

PRO TIP: Check out the alley alongside the Blue Mouse Theatre. It has a mural of the many films that made the Blue Mouse iconic, including the poster for *The Green Goddess.*

BEAR PIT

Did a grizzly bear escape from a Tacoma park?

Yep. Point Defiance is incredible. It's a more than 720-acre park here in Tacoma. It began its life, of course, as Puyallup tribal territory, but then became a federal military reserve before being turned over in 1888 to the City of Tacoma. One of the wildest things about it is the bear pit. In 1899, the parks department decided to put a zoo here. By zoo, I mean bear pit. The first bears afforded, as you might guess, casual encounters for visitors. The part that truly surprises many people is that in 1937 a male grizzly bear was brought to the park and jumped the fence, which wasn't much of a fence. The bear then vanished. Two volunteers, Howard and Happy, were dispatched, Jurassic Park–style, out into the woods with high-powered rifles. They tracked the bear to the edge of the park and found that it had vanished into the city. It was never seen again. That's the part that gets me.

A DERELICT ZOO

WHAT: An old bear pit, minus one wily bear

WHERE: Alongside the rose garden in Point Defiance Park

COST: Free

PRO TIP: Don't forget to visit the unsung hero of Point Defiance, the Northwest Native Plant Garden. This collection of native plants is near the former bear pit and is a wonderful retreat.

Point Defiance didn't just have bears, it also had elk. One of which had such massive antlers that in 1903 they were used to make a chair for President Theodore Roosevelt.

Apparently, in 1937, a grizzly bear just wandered off into Tacoma, and we never saw him again. If anybody sees this bear or has any information leading to its capture, please let me know. If you come to Point Defiance today, you can see a lot of things, including the new zoo, which is way better than a bear pit. However, for the truly curious, you can still see the remnants of the old bear pit, or more specifically the waterfall grotto from the bear pit, located right here on the edge of the rose garden.

Photo courtesy of Tacoma Public Library

RAILROAD HQ

Where does the region's most powerful railroad call home?

The main building for the Northern Pacific Railroad was first located in downtown Tacoma on what is now St. Helens Street. However, as the power and class of Tacoma grew, so did the power of the railroad. They quickly decided they needed not only more space but a better vantage. Tacoma was tied, more than anything else, to the fortunes of the railroad, and as the Northern Pacific wanted to show the world how impressive they were, they needed a building to match. That's why in 1888 they opened their new headquarters building that was iconic for the region. It was built in the classic Italian style and was perched on the cliff overlooking both Commencement Bay and Half Moon Yard. Half Moon Yard was long considered the largest switching yard west of the Mississippi River. In essence, it was an area where the trains could switch cars and cargo. The railroad executives wanted to keep an eye on the whole process and all the money they would be making, so the elegant headquarters had to

THE HEADQUARTERS OF TRANSPORTATION

WHAT: Once the most important building in Tacoma

WHERE: One Pacific Building, 621 Pacific Ave.

COST: Free

PRO TIP: The view from below the building is amazing and can be best seen from along the waterfront by Thea Foss Park.

The roof of the Northern Pacific Headquarters had a setup to expose photosensitive blueprinting paper to hand-drawn plans, charts, and maps. Essentially, it was a sun-powered copy station on the roof.

be close. The building was built to have 53 offices and storerooms aligned with a reported 19 vaults for the variety of companies that would also lease space from the railroad. Not only were the railroad executives working inside the headquarters, so were other powerful groups like the Tacoma Land Company and the timber barons at the Weyerhaeuser Company. This made it arguably the most important and powerful building in all of Tacoma. As the railroad fell out of power and companies like Weyerhaeuser moved away, the prominence of the railroad headquarters diminished.

Today it is called the One Pacific Building, and it has office space for lease.

TOP OF THE OCEAN

Was one of Tacoma's most famous restaurants actually a boat?

Top of the Ocean was an iconic part of the Tacoma waterfront for generations. This famous restaurant opened in 1946, and the people who built it had the local shipwrights construct it as if it were actually a ship, but it was really just a restaurant on a dock. The illusion was pretty convincing, and several people who lived in Tacoma at the time swear to this day that they once saw Top of the Ocean sail away. The Top was a legend on Ruston Way until April 1977 when it was burned to the ground. Or, rather, it was burned to the waterline.

Photo courtesy of Tacoma Public Library

The police solved the case almost instantly because the arsonist was so sloppy. He was a man named David Levage. Levage got a cab to drive him down to Top of the Ocean the night of the arson and asked the driver to help him unload a box of liquid. The next day, the police found eight empty one-gallon containers of paint thinner that had been used as an accelerant for the arson.

FORMER NIGHTLIFE HOTSPOT

WHAT: A monument to one of Tacoma's quirkiest restaurants

WHERE: 2211 Ruston Way

COST: Free

PRO TIP: Grab some fish and chips next door at the Northern Fish Co. A true Tacoma legend, they've been in business since 1912.

The cab driver, named Richard Black, was watching the news that morning and immediately thought of the man he had driven to the Top of the Ocean the night before. Richard called it in, and the police arrested Levage soon after. His fingerprints were all over the empty cans of paint thinner. This was all truly just the tip of the iceberg because the arrest of Levage unfurled a whole criminal conspiracy. By the end of the investigation, it had been determined that Levage was an arsonist for a crime boss named John Carbone. The burning of the Top of the Ocean led to the conviction of not only Levage but also John Carbone, the local sheriff George Janovich, and 12 others.

Metro Parks finally added a small bronze model of the former Top of the Ocean on the site of the former restaurant. A little memorial to what was once the greatest restaurant in Tacoma.

TACOMA DOME

Is the world's largest wooden dome in Tacoma?

Tacoma is home to one of the largest wooden domes in the world. This magnificent piece of architecture is only dwarfed by the Superior Dome in Michigan. The Superior Dome is 536 feet in diameter, and the Tacoma Dome is 530 feet in diameter. This is why the record books will tell you that the Tacoma Dome is only the *second* largest wooden dome in the world, but the mighty Tacoma Dome is nine feet taller than the Superior Dome and holds 5,000 more people. So I would argue that Tacoma's grandest events space is actually the bigger of the two. Regardless, the Tacoma Dome's journey to its current home was an explosive one. Back in May 1980 Mount St. Helens erupted with a force that moved at 670 miles per hour at one point. This eruption leveled miles of old-growth forest.

ICONIC VENUE ON THE TACOMA SKYLINE

WHAT: *Maybe* the world's largest dome

WHERE: 2727 E D St.

COST: Depends on the event

PRO TIP: If you think it's going to be busy at the Dome, you can park downtown and take the T Line light rail from one of the stations and get off near the Tacoma Dome.

These trees were salvaged by the Weyerhaeuser Timber family and supplied for the construction of the Tacoma Dome. The wooden roof weighs 1.44 million pounds and is made of 288 hand-nailed and prefabricated triangular units called glulams (glue-LAMS).

When the Tacoma Dome was conceived, a space had to be found for it, and the Hawthorne neighborhood was selected. Not everyone was happy about the decision, though. The City of Tacoma offered to buy and then demolish or move every home in the neighborhood to make way for the Dome, but

Photo courtesy of Tacoma Public Library

some citizens, like longtime resident Erik Johnson, mounted a vigorous rebellion against relocation. He and everyone else in the neighborhood eventually lost out, and the Dome went in. Several of the homes were lifted onto flatbed trucks and even barges to be moved. Today the Tacoma Dome remains one of the most iconic venues in the Pacific Northwest and an indelible part of the Tacoma skyline.

The colorful neon lights that are part of the interior decor had originally been suggested to adorn the exterior of the dome.

FREIGHTHOUSE SQUARE

Is Tacoma's funkiest shopping center an old train depot?

Once considered the longest freight warehouse in the US, this structure is now home to an eclectic collection of shops and restaurants. The Milwaukee Railroad was doing a tremendous amount of business in Tacoma during the early 1900s and was very excited to be connected to the Port of Tacoma. They wanted a storage facility for their shipped goods, though, and so a freight warehouse was planned. By 1909, the 540-by-50-foot structure was open for business and the Chicago, Milwaukee, St. Paul and Pacific Railroad had a base for storing goods in the Tacoma area. In 1941, an addition made the freight warehouse even longer.

Today the space is measured to have approximately 108,000 square feet. When the Milwaukee Railroad was in full operation, they would have used the freight house for storage and as a corporate office. In fact, it was the division headquarters for the West Coast. Sadly, air-cargo transportation eclipsed the railroad by the 1970s and the freight house looked like it was done for. Then in 1987 a local entrepreneur named Keith Stone bought the building and opened it with the fitting branding of Freighthouse Square.

The trains still stop at Freighthouse Square. It remains a station for the Sounder commuter train as well as the Amtrak.

There have been ups and downs, and the success of the space has been as wild as the success of the early railroad. Today you can find some of Tacoma's most beloved restaurants and so many small local vendors that you'll be blown away. There are candy shops, gift shops, art galleries, and game shops, just to name a few. With an ever-rotating cast in a charming historic spot along the commuter train rail line and its being the train station for the Amtrak, there is always an adventure to be had in historic Freighthouse Square.

FORMER FREIGHT HOUSE

WHAT: An eclectic collection of local shops and markets in a former train station

WHERE: 2501 E D St.

COST: The cost of a coffee or a lunch

PRO TIP: If you're looking for a gift for that difficult-to-shop-for person, this is your place. It is a wild market with great flair.

Photo courtesy of Tacoma Public Library

NATIONAL GUARD TRAINING FACILITY

WHAT: A former armory building turned into an arts center

WHERE: 1001 S Yakima Ave.

COST: Depends on the event

PRO TIP: Try to visit on a night that there is roller-skating. Hitting that drill floor with your skates on is the coolest.

ARMORY

Did a former armory host the Prince of Norway?

The Tacoma Armory building was constructed in 1908, opened in 1909, and has played host to several significant events in Tacoma's history. It has not only been used to train the State Guard but was also influential in boxing matches, hockey matches, garden expos, and once hosted the Prince of Norway.

World War I gave the US an excellent opportunity to muster a fighting force and prove to the world that we were a nation to be contended with. The drill floors were large open spaces that were used for artillery drilling. On the drill floor soldiers would practice the motion of loading, firing, and reloading so that it would be second nature to them in conflict situations.

The downstairs of the armory was used for the cavalry. It had a stable and firing range. In the basement there is also a low boiler room with a deep pool section. This was used as a horse bath for the military horses. Over time, the armory was also used to host events like political rallies and expos. The large drill floor made an excellent space for gatherings that needed either heat or a roof.

Today the armory is an events center that hosts some of the great expos and arts of Tacoma.

Photo courtesy of Tacoma Public Library

Music was a huge part of the armory's history as well. Concerts have been played inside, and several bands, including the Wailers, performed inside. During Tacoma's Norwegian Festival in 1939, Prince Olav of Norway visited with his wife. From boxing matches to political rallies, the armory has always been there to host the city. At one point in the 1980s the armory became an overflow center for the local jailhouse. Metal cells were temporarily constructed inside the armory, and prisoners were held inside while Pierce County expanded their facilities.

TACOMA'S STREETCAR DISASTER

How did a Fourth of July celebration turn deadly?

One of the deadliest disasters in Tacoma's history took place in July 1900. It was a rainy morning in Tacoma, and people were excited to celebrate the Fourth of July and usher in a new century. The Tacoma Railway and Power Company had assigned a trolley from the Point Defiance line to go and gather people from South Tacoma. Despite the dreary weather, there was a crowd of more than 50,000 people gathering in downtown Tacoma, and streetcar No. 116 was already looking overcrowded by 8 a.m. The rain made things worse because few people were interested in walking, and the tracks were becoming slick in the slippery conditions.

One of the riders recalled that people were packed in so tightly that he couldn't reach down to get a dime from his pocket for the fare. As the streetcar approached the steep Delin Street grade, it quickly veered out of control. The car needed to take a sharp left turn along the edge of a deep 100-foot ravine, but the combination of the slippery tracks, the overloaded car, and the inexperience of the young motorman, F. Boehm, led to the car jumping the tracks and rolling violently down the ravine. More than 40 people were killed in the accident.

Police, firefighters, doctors, and nurses were quick to respond, but the steep sides of the ravine made rescue efforts difficult. Even when rescue workers could get to the bottom, it was challenging, if not impossible, to carry the wounded out.

Tacoma has a streetcar today that travels through the city, but it follows a much safer route.

REMOVING THE DEAD BODIES FROM THE WRECK.

Photo courtesy of newspapers.com, The Tacoma Daily Ledger

In the end, the official records stated that there were 43 dead passengers and 65 wounded or maimed. It was the deadliest transportation accident in the city at the time. Today there is a small marker memorializing those who lost their lives.

MEMORIAL SITE FOR TRANSPORTATION TRAGEDY

WHAT: One of the deadliest transportation disasters in Washington history

WHERE: At the bottom of the Delin Street Bridge

COST: Free

PRO TIP: If you want to try a safer ride, the Link Lightrail (our new streetcar) in Tacoma runs from the Tacoma Dome station to St. Joseph's Hospital and is an excellent way to see the city.

PAUPER'S FIELD CEMETERY

BURIAL GROUND FOR THE UNKNOWN

WHAT: An all but forgotten cemetery

WHERE: 5202 S Junett St.

COST: Free

PRO TIP: The surrounding area houses Tacoma's earliest cemeteries. Take an hour and explore the South Park and Tacoma Cemetery area.

Is one of the area's largest cemeteries unmarked?

On the far end of the Tacoma Cemetery is what appears to be a quiet field. Upon closer inspection, you may notice a handful of rough stone markers peeking out of the tall grass. This two-acre plot is actually not an undeveloped lot but the Pauper's Cemetery or Pauper's Field. It is a cemetery that was donated to the county by the Northern Pacific Railroad and has become the final resting place for roughly 1,800 individuals who were either

anonymous or too poor when they died to be buried with a proper marker and service. In some cases, if the undertaker knew that there would be multiple burials in a single day, he wouldn't dig a new grave but would leave the first one open and bury individuals two to three deep in a single plot. Several of Tacoma's first pioneers and visiting sailors would be laid to rest in Pauper's Field only to be forgotten with time.

Tacoma had four funeral homes at the time and each would take a three-month turn burying the dead. The county would pay them $4.50 per burial for the service and the coffin.

Today the tall grass covers the handful of markers that remain, and only the legends and ghost stories of the region keep watch over the almost 2,000 individuals who were buried here in Tacoma's earliest days.

Of the few headstones that exist in Pauper's Field, many are written in Japanese or Chinese, as this was also the cemetery for Tacoma's earliest populations from both Japan and China.

TACOMA NARROWS

Is there a national historic place underwater?

The Tacoma Narrows Bridge was the third-longest suspension bridge in the world when it opened on July 1, 1940. Just a few short months later, on November 7, it would collapse in high winds. "Galloping Gertie" was the most dramatic bridge collapse in American history. The wreckage of the bridge, roadway and all, fell to the frigid depths of the Tacoma Narrows, some 180 feet down.

Over time, the tons of concrete and steel became more than just a reminder of that dramatic day. They became a reef for an abundance of marine life in the region. The giant Pacific octopus, in particular, has come to rely on the protection and excellent hunting grounds the reef provides. To prevent salvagers from dredging up and removing the part of the Tacoma Narrows Bridge on the floor of Puget Sound, several historians moved to have the site added to the National Register of Historic

THE MOST FAMOUS BRIDGE IN WASHINGTON

WHAT: The wreckage of the Tacoma Narrows Bridge

WHERE: About 180 feet underwater

COST: Dive lessons and years of training

PRO TIP: You can see some amazing documentaries from the dive expeditions that have made it to the bottom over the years. It's a much safer way to explore the ruins. Or you could watch the short film *The Lost Angle*, which looks at lost footage of the bridge collapse and is narrated by me!

There was only one fatality from the 1940 collapse of the Narrows Bridge. It was a black cocker spaniel named Tubby, who some sources swear had only three legs.

Places. They were successful. In 1992, the wreckage of the Narrows Bridge was officially added.

Diving to the site is incredibly dangerous and can be attempted only by the most talented and well-equipped divers. Those who make the descent, though, are greeted by a truly wondrous sight and can explore the now protected ruins in the dark depths of the Narrows.

Photo courtesy of Tacoma Public Library

TACOMA'S SEA MONSTER

What would you do if you were attacked by a sea monster that could shoot electric arcs?

THE DAILY LEDGER, TACOMA, WASHIN[illegible]

A SEA-SERPENT SEEN.

It was Discovered Yesterday in Tacoma Waters.

ONE OF THE OCEAN'S MONSTERS.

Scores Gaze in Wonder at the Point Where It Went Down.

It was at first thought to be nothing but a tangled mass of seaweed floating in the water. Closer inspection, however, disclosed the fact that the object was a genuine sea-serpent, a veritable monster of the deep. By accurate eye measurement the serpent was at least thirty-five feet long and four feet thick, tapering gradually from the shoulders down to the tail like a fish. It is undoubtedly the first of its species ever seen in Tacoma waters and the following description of the beast is furnished by the gentleman who saw it.

The creature was part horse, part fish and part saurian. About the upper part of its head and face it greatly resembled the ordinary farm horse, the face being full and oval in shape. The head was nearly five feet long, the most peculiar feature being the eyes. They were out of all proportion to the head, the balls being of a bright red color, resembling in size and shape the Holland cheese of commerce. When angered the serpent's eyes hung out on its face and emitted sparks of green fire. Its ears grew close to its head, but could be thrown forward and back like those of a jackass in the act of listening.

The cut of its mouth and in fact the whole lower part of its face denoted cruelty and savage cunning. When the serpent yawned, which it frequently did, its mouth was exactly like the circus poster portrait of the celebrated blood-sweating Bohemeth of Holy writ, which wades far out into the water, utters a low, plaintive cry and wades back again, for reasons best known to itself. Its teeth were black and very sharp, growing in three rows on each jaw. The nostrils were placed diagonally across the lower

Photo courtesy of newspapers.com, The Tacoma Daily Ledger

In 1893, the first recorded account of the Tacoma serpent was published when two fishermen, R. E. McClean and W. J. Kennedy, claimed to have been attacked by a monster that was no less than 150 feet in length, with shining copper bands and rolling dark eyes. The fishermen claimed that when they were attempting to haul the creature out of the sea it discharged a strong bolt of electricity and shocked them, knocking one of the fishermen unconscious.

The original account quotes a fisherman. He said he saw a "demon of the deep." He goes on to describe it as "fully 150 feet long with a head like a walrus and six large, round eyes the size of dinner plates."

The account goes on: "instantly the whole air was filled with a strong current of electricity that caused every nerve in the body to sting with pain, and a light as bright as that created by the concentration of many arc lights kept constantly flashing. At first I thought it was a thunderstorm, but as no rain accompanied it, and as both light and sound came from off the bay, I turned my head in that direction, and if it is possible for fright to turn one's hair white, then mine ought to be snow white, for right before my eyes was a most horrible-looking monster."

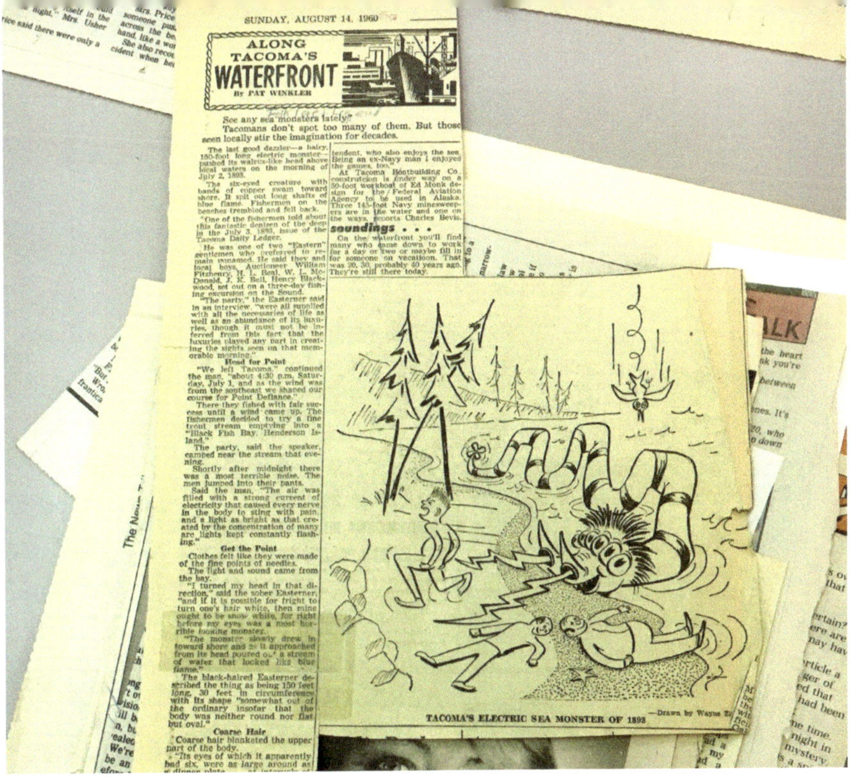

To this day, no giant serpents with mastery over electricity have been hauled ashore in Tacoma, or at least none that we know of. The closest thing is the King-of-the-Salmon, a species of ribbon fish that can sometimes be found in Puget sound and does grow to be more than six feet long.

THE SEA SERPENT

WHAT: Tacoma's very own sea monster

WHERE: Some 200 feet below the waterline

COST: A day spent fishing

PRO TIP: The original account states that the sea serpent loves minnows. If you're going fishing for a local legend, you'll need lots of bait and some very strong fishing line.

Puget Sound may or may not have a giant serpent in it, but it absolutely has several Steller sea lions. Male Steller sea lions can grow to be 10 feet long and weigh 2,400 pounds, which is basically a sea monster for all our kayakers.

HORSE TRACK CENTER

Was one of Tacoma's nicest neighborhoods once a center for gambling and vice?

It may not look like it now, but the Proctor Neighborhood was once a center for illegal gambling and backstreet deals. The lord of crime Harry Morgan was Tacoma's most notorious vice king in the 1800s. By the time Tacoma was selected to be the terminus for the transcontinental railroad's northern route, Morgan had put down roots in Tacoma and made sure there were enough saloons, gambling halls, and brothels for the sailors and working men who came through town.

FORMER RACETRACK

WHAT: One of Tacoma's most important racetracks

WHERE: What is now the Proctor Neighborhood

COST: Free

PRO TIP: As you explore the Proctor Neighborhood, don't forget to look down. The historical society has worked hard to have bronze plaques installed in the sidewalk with the history of the buildings and area printed on them.

The City of Tacoma pushed Morgan to the fringes of Tacoma. Harry wanted to open a large track for racing and gambling, so he went farther out. Tacoma already had a professional racetrack south of town, but the Tacoma Driving Park was sold in 1888 and Harry wanted to control the action. In 1890 he began the construction of a one-mile track with a 120-stall barn in the woods. Today the same location would be the Proctor Neighborhood from approximately North 25th Street and

Tacoma has a long history of racing. It used to be home to the Tacoma Speedway, which hosted the biggest car races on the West Coast from 1914 to 1922.

TROTTING AND RUNNING

Second Day of the Races at the Tacoma Speeding Park.

A MUCH LARGER ATTENDANCE.

Misty Morn, Pandora, Kitty Hamm and Pat Cunen the Winners—To-Day's Programme.

The attendance at the races was considerably larger yesterday than on the opening day. The grand stand held also a good many ladies who are interested in racing. Among them were noticed Mrs. Stuart Rice, Mrs. Anderson, Mrs. Hosmer and Mrs. John S. Baker. The racing also was a considerable improvement over the first day. A gentleman interested in racing said that a better race was never run on the track than the 2:26 trotting class. The races were as follows:

Fifth race, Breeders' stake for 2-year-olds, horses owned in Washington, Oregon, Idaho, Montana and British Columbia. Misty Morn (R. S. Bybee, Portland), Laurette (W. L. Whitmore, Portland). Won by Misty Morn; time, 1:07.

Sixth race, 3-year-old trotting, one mile, best two in three heats, purse $300. Pandora (T. S. Tongue, Portland), Cœur d'Alene (S. G. Reed, Portland). First heat won by Pandora, time 2:49¼; second heat won by Pandora, time 2:37½.

Seventh race, 2:26, trotting, open to all, best 3 in 5 heats, in harness; purse, $450—Alto, (F. Enos, Portland); Kittie Hamm, (T. Tongue, Portland); Blondie, (Von De Lashmult, Portland); Joe Kennie, (J. M. Dougan, Tacoma). First heat, won by Kittie Hamm; time, 2:28. Second heat, won by Joe Kennie; time, 2:26¾. Third heat, Kittie Hamm; time, 2:26¼. Fourth heat, Kittie Hamm; time, 2:29¼. Alto went lame and Blondie was distanced, and Kittie Hamm was awarded first and third money; Joe Kinnie second money.

Special running race, open to all, one mile dash; purse, $150—J. M. R., (Ed Fortune); Pat Cunen, (W. L. Whitmore); Oceanica, (R. M. Bybee). Won by Pat Cunen; time, 1:49; J. M. R., second, Oceanic, third.

To-day's programme is:

Ninth race, one and one-fourth miles, running, purse $400—Veanica (R. S. By-

Photo courtesy of newspapers.com, The Tacoma Daily Ledger

North Proctor Street all the way to North 15th Street and North Union Avenue. Morgan never got to see the fruits of his labor, though. In April of 1890, Morgan died. The official cause of death was listed as heart failure, but there was speculation that it was an opium overdose.

The racetrack was sold to the police chief Matt Dillon, who made his fortune taking illegal payoffs from Morgan. Dillon named the track the Morgan Memorial Speedway. It was in operation by July 1890. By 1902, the track failed and the cheap land and clear-cut sections now connected to streetcar lines made for an easy transition to the Proctor Neighborhood. The next time you're standing outside Metropolitan Market, just remember the seedy den of sin and corruption this used to be.

MONKEYSHINES

Do anonymous artists host an annual treasure hunt?

Every Lunar New Year, Tacoma goes all out with one of the most beloved traditions in the county. We call them monkeyshines. Monkeyshines can be medallions or glass floats, but they all come stamped with the corresponding animal of that year's Chinese zodiac. In 2004, a local artist known as Ms. Monkey began the tradition of hiding glass art through Tacoma.

The connection to Lunar New Year was a happy accident, though. She had intended to hide glass floats through the city for Christmas, but the process was time-consuming and got delayed until about the Lunar New Year of 2004. Ms. Monkey had a close friend who had a bronze stamp embossed with a monkey face that was chosen as the seal for the glass art she was blowing. That year just happened to be the year of the monkey, and so destiny was sealed. Every year now Ms. Monkey and the monkeys make more than 2,000 free pieces of glass art and stamp them with a bronze animal stamp. A dedicated team of mysterious volunteers then undergoes the task of hiding the monkeyshines throughout Tacoma.

Each year they are hidden in places that get you to explore and appreciate the city. If you find one, you get to keep it because it brings you good fortune and good luck.

The monkeys generally start hiding these floats throughout the community around midnight on Lunar New Year, although it's always a mystery where and when. Of course,

---

Many people will re-hide monkeyshines from previous years. This is OK, but you should never give one away or your good luck may go with it.

the community also gets together and hides "rogues" or unofficial treasures throughout the area. These rogues can be anything from miniature figurines to painted art—anything that celebrates the animal of the year. It's one of my absolute favorite traditions for the area and is a wonderful and exciting way to get to know Tacoma.

BELOVED LOCAL TRADITON

WHAT: A great annual treasure hunt

WHERE: All throughout Tacoma

COST: Free

PRO TIP: While there is never any way to know where the monkeys will hide the monkeyshines, they tend to always hide them around Lunar New Year and in public locations. You will never need to break into public property or climb on something dangerous to get one. That said, sometimes you may need to swim.

TACOMA'S MOST HAUNTED SPACE

WHAT: A haunted series of rooms that watch over the city

WHERE: The third floor of 703 Pacific Ave.

COST: However much it would be to repair and remediate the third floor to get it ready for a lease

PRO TIP: Check out the glass tiles in the sidewalk in front of the building. They are part of the original underground vault lights and show what it used to look like in Tacoma's first days as a modern city.

HAUNTED BRADLEY

Why was this central downtown space abandoned?

There is a building in downtown Tacoma teeming with ghostly stories. This unassuming building is part of the Bodega Court, a series of buildings that were constructed after Tacoma was selected to become a railroad boomtown. The Northern Pacific Railroad constructed their new headquarters on Pacific Avenue and had city hall built across the street. The main avenue leading out their front doorstep became known as Whiskey Row over the years, the main zone for saloons and dens of vice.

One of the most profitable saloons was the Bodegea Court, established in 1889. It would have been located in the building that Meconi's occupies today. As a part of this empire, though, there were several brothels along the way, including the third floor of 703 Pacific Avenue. This spot allegedly operated from the 1890s until 1952, when it was shut down and abandoned. That's the last time there was a tenant on the third floor.

Some of the building's previous occupants have said they have heard the sound of something large being dragged across the floor, but the brave few who have dared go up the stairs have only found the abandoned furniture that was left in the rooms after the place was shut down. To this day, it remains the only part of the building without an occupant—well, at least no living occupants.

The whole of Whiskey Row, where the Bradley is located, has the highest concentration of ghost stories in all of Tacoma.

TACOMA'S MISSING TOTEM POLE

Was Tacoma's tallest tourist attraction a fake?

There was a totem pole that used to reside here from 1903 until August 2021.

It's a complicated story. In 1899, Seattle took its chamber of commerce up to Alaska, where they encountered a Tlingit village in Fort Tongass, when the tribe was away fishing.

With no one there to stop them, the chamber found a sacred totem pole in the village and chopped it down. The men put it on their ship and erected the pole in Pioneer Square. The city of Seattle had an unveiling in October of 1899.

Tacoma, which has long been a rival of Seattle, seized this opportunity to strike Seattle's reputation and to boost their own. Arctic explorer and local Tacoma booster William F. Sheard suggested that the world's largest totem pole be crafted for the city, not stolen. Sheard and Tacoma banker Chester Thorne combined their powers and raised more than $3,000 to have the world's largest totem pole erected in the city of Tacoma. William said he would find an Alaskan native from one of the tribes up north to carve it and deliver it to Tacoma. However, two anonymous artisans on Vashon Island carved the totem pole. It was set up in May 1903 in downtown Tacoma, where it stood for more than 100 years.

Tacoma no longer hosts a totem pole, but it does have a welcome pole, or story pole. The figure stands by Tollefson Plaza and is a modern take on the traditional art form made by local Puyallup artist Qwalsius (Shaun Peterson).

Photo courtesy of Tacoma Public Library

LOCAL TOTEM POLE

WHAT: Tacoma's former totem pole, once the tallest in the world

WHERE: In hiding for now

COST: Free

PRO TIP: Head down to Firefighter's Park and see the new art, *Swell*, which is meant to honor the history in Tacoma. The piece is interactive, so if you stand in the middle it looks like the two men on it are pulling aside the edge of the 11th Street Bridge to reveal Mount Rainier.

There is a catch, though. As confirmed by Dr. Robin Wright of University of Washington, the totem pole didn't match any of the styles or artistry of any of the Alaskan tribes or of the Coast Salish people. So where did it come from? Over time, people came to discover that the Tacoma totem pole was forged.

The decision was eventually made that the totem pole needed to come down and be replaced with some representative Coast Salish art. In August 2021 the totem pole was taken down.

MISSING SAFE

How much is a missing safe worth these days?

One of my favorite Tacoma stories is about a missing safe with $14,000 inside that to this day no one has been able to locate. In November 1894, when an earthquake hit the region, 300 yards of Tacoma waterfront slid into Commencement Bay in an instant. This included several railroad offices, the payroll safe, the guardhouses, and even homes. In all the destruction, two lives were lost. Fourteen-year-old Emma Stubbs was inside her home in her bed when the entire building slid into the water and she drowned inside. Her body was never recovered.

John Hansen was the guard for the payroll office that night, and as the building came unmoored from the shore and

A LOST PAYROLL SAFE

WHAT: A missing safe with $500,000 inside

WHERE: That's a good question

COST: How much is a dive team?

PRO TIP: The safe was last seen along the shore by where the TEMCO grain silos are today.

Area where the safe went missing
Photo courtesy of Tacoma Public Library

crashed into the icy November water, John Hansen went with it. Most people believed that he drowned inside the building, and the payroll safe vanished to the murky depths below. A huge search was undertaken by the railroad, which wanted to get its $14,000 back. That would be about $500,000 in today's money. The search team eventually recovered Hansen's body, and the payroll office was actually found miles away in Quartermaster Harbor on Vashon Island. The safe, however, was no longer attached to the building. Over the years, multiple people have looked for the safe to no avail. Treasure hunters and amateur detectives have spent years looking for clues and using side scan sonar to try and locate the safe, but its location and its contents remain lost to time and tide.

Local salvage experts haven't found the missing safe, but they did recover an anchor that had been lost from one of the earliest tall ships in the area.

CHARLOTTE'S FREE BLUEBERRY PARK

Is there a free park where you can pick all the blueberries you want?

There is a 23-acre urban oasis in Tacoma that has more than 4,000 blueberry plants and five varieties of blueberry inside.

It began as a 53-acre farm in the 1920s. Lars and Gina Berg ran a blueberry farm with their son from 1952 until 1968. The Bergs hailed from North Dakota, where they grew wheat, but when they arrived to Tacoma they took a chance on the dense and rich peaty soil. The blueberry farm thrived for years. In the late '60s the Bergs sold the land to Tacoma School District #10. The school had planned to build a new high school there, but the community was fully opposed.

The neighborhood loved the blueberries, and several of the people who lived nearby had grown up as kids and students hired by the Berg family to pick the berries during peak season. The school district listened and instead traded more than 20 acres to Tacoma Parks for a portion of Manitou Park, where they could build an elementary school.

When the parks department took over the 23 acres, they had the choice of developing an area with fields and play equipment or keeping the legacy of this place alive. They chose right. In 1997 the park was opened as Blueberry Park and is maintained by a team of volunteers who tend the more than 4,000 plants.

If you really want to double down, you can also find a massive amount of local blackberries in the region that are free to pick as well.

The park itself is now a multipurpose area, both a free blueberry farm as well as a protected wetland that provides habitat for a huge array of animals and helps to clean the water of pollutants before it returns to the ground reserves.

The name was changed in 2010 from Blueberry Park to Charlotte's Blueberry Park in honor of longtime volunteer and berry advocate Charlotte Valbert.

BLUEBERRIES FOR THE PUBLIC

WHAT: A park full of free blueberries for you to pick

WHERE: 7402 E D St.

COST: Free

PRO TIP: Consider bringing some gloves or a bag for weeds. It's not required but certainly appreciated if you pull a couple weeds when you go and get your blueberries.

NEVER NEVER LAND STATUES

How do you get a rat to run up a clock?

In the summer of 1964, the fairytale-themed attraction known as Never Never Land Park opened in Point Defiance. This park had life-sized fiberglass statues of popular fairytales. There were the three little pigs, the old woman in the shoe, and Jack and Jill, just to name a few. Never Never Land was the creation of Alfred Petterson. He was an artist who had opened a similar park in Victoria, British Columbia, called Wooded Wonderland. The Canadian park had been wonderfully successful, so Petterson moved to Tacoma to try again. Never Never Land was a hit, and soon throngs of enchanted children passed under the storybook entrance and waved to the 8-foot-tall Humpty Dumpty that perched atop the entrance, smiling down at them.

Photo courtesy of Tacoma Public Library

One of the most iconic attractions inside was the Hickory Dickory Clock. Children could push a button and the mouse would run up the clock. Well, a rat would. The rats were Long Evans hooded males. The general manager, James Ruder, trained each rat by hand so that when the button was pushed, a small door would open and the rats would run to the top to get a small piece of food.

Petterson went on to open another park in Ontario and had plans to make even more, but the success of the original parks proved hard to replicate. Some of the statues Petterson made ended up in the vaulted sidewalk section of downtown businesses like Meconi's. These abandoned statues gathered dust and ghost stories in the darkness below the streets of Tacoma.

Tacoma's Never Never Land Park stayed open from 1964 until 2001. After that, a few lingering statues haunted the trails until the area was fully closed by Metro Parks in 2010. The remaining statues, including those below the street downtown, went up for auction.

A BELOVED CHILDHOOD TRADITION

WHAT: A fairytale-themed park that used to be in Point Defiance

WHERE: The trails behind Fort Nisqually

COST: Free

PRO TIP: You can still find a few of the former figures for sale along Antique Row in Tacoma. The parks department auctioned off the last of their major figures a while ago, but private collectors are holding on to some in Tacoma today.

Even though the statues are gone, you can still visit the site where Never Never Land used to be. Follow the trails behind Fort Nisqually off 5 Mile Drive.

THE MOUNTAINEER TREE

TACOMA'S NATURAL WONDER

WHAT: Tacoma's oldest tree

WHERE: Along 5 Mile Dr., right before the Dalco Passage Viewpoint

COST: Free

PRO TIP: There are miles of trails in Point Defiance Park, and they weave all through the old-growth forest. It makes for a wonderful day trip for anyone looking to get out of the urban environment without leaving the city.

Where is Tacoma's oldest tree?

The tallest and oldest tree in all of Tacoma is in Point Defiance Park. The Mountaineer Tree is estimated to be about 450 years old and is currently 218 feet tall, with a trunk that is approximately 24 feet around. It is a stunning reminder of the old-growth forests that used to dominate the landscape we now call Tacoma. Before the lumber industry changed the skyline forever, these giants were the norm. Point Defiance survived the lumberjack's axe by briefly being designated as a military site and then was turned over to the City of Tacoma for use as a park. Some of the branches are larger in diameter than the 30-year-old Douglas fir trees down below.

The Mountaineers are a climbing group that celebrates the natural wonder of the world. The Tacoma branch of the Mountaineers was founded in 1912. When a group of Tacoma Mountaineers, led by Carl Heaton, in 1949 noticed the grandeur of the tree, they moved to make sure it was protected and celebrated, thus the reason it is known as the

People often say that Point Defiance is the largest urban park in America. It isn't, but it is a really big one.

Mountaineer Tree. At 450 years old (we think), it would have been alive at the time William Shakespeare was writing some of his best-known plays.

HERBERT DUNE PARK

Was a toxic dump turned into a city park?

One of the wildest parts of Tacoma is Dune Peninsula Park, named after Tacoma native Frank Herbert, the author of the Dune series. It may look like a simple peninsula with a park on top, but it is so much more. Right next door for about 100 years was the ASARCO smelting plant, which specialized in refining raw copper. One of the byproducts of that was a tremendous amount of arsenic and molten lead, as well as other toxic materials. The ASARCO plant wanted a way to get rid of that toxic material. Their solution was to dump it in Puget Sound. They dumped so much that they created a nice little peninsula right next door, a convenient breakwater for the Tacoma Yacht Club.

Tons of lead slag piled up along the shoreline. As the years went on, the ASARCO smelter was embroiled in controversy with the new Environmental Protection Agency. When ASARCO finally shut down, the City of Tacoma and Ruston had a dilemma on their hands. How do you clean up 100-plus years of pollution? The City of Tacoma along with Metro Parks developed a remediation plan that would cap 100 years of toxic material to prevent it from flowing out into the ocean and then put a park essentially right on top of it.

LOCAL PARK WITH A DARK PAST

WHAT: A stunning waterfront park on top of a toxic dump

WHERE: 5361 Yacht Club Rd.

COST: Free

PRO TIP: On the edge of the park there is a massive bucket-shaped item that many people think is a bell. It's actually one of the old crucibles used to hold molten lead and arsenic as it was pulled out from ASARCO on a local train line and tipped into the sound.

The name for the park, Dune Peninsula Park, was chosen because Frank Herbert's Dune series addresses the environmental impact politics and capitalism have on our world. Having grown up in Tacoma, Herbert used to reference his time coming of age next to the ASARCO smelter as influential to his body of work.

In the middle of the park there are bronze sculptures of juvenile sand worms, the iconic creatures from *Dune*. These ones are easier to ride.

UFOS IN TACOMA

Is the truth out there in Washington?

In the summer of 1947, there were several events that immortalized UFOs in the public mind forever. On June 21, 1947, a local salvage ship captain, Harold Dahl, had an experience aboard his boat the *North Queen* when he arrived off the edge of Maury Island. There he was confronted by six flying discs overhead. According to Dahl, one of the discs began spewing hot white sheets of "newspaper-like material" and molten rock. The hot material landed on Harold's ship. The next day, Dahl claimed he was approached by a man in a dark suit and told not to talk about the event. The man said he knew what Dahl had seen in the water and warned him not to tell anyone or bad things might happen. Dahl's account is our first modern reference to the men in black.

Then, on June 24, just three days after Dahl's sighting off Maury Island, a local pilot named Kenneth Arnold claimed to see nine objects flying near Mount Rainier. Arnold went so far as to coin the term "flying saucer" in describing the movement of the objects he saw. This is extra remarkable when you consider that the Roswell incident happened on July 8 of the same year. From there, Arnold got in touch with Lieutenant Frank Brown of Military Intelligence, who flew to the area to meet at Arnold's hotel, the Winthrop, in Tacoma, along with Captain William Davidson of the US Air Corps.

Every year in June some parts of the community still have a celebration to commemorate the men in black and the UFOs in Tacoma.

Davidson and Brown came to investigate the Maury Island incident and what happened off the coast here. They conducted interviews, collected fragments, and then readied to return to California, but in the early hours of August 1, their B-25 crashed outside of Kelso, Washington, killing both men. This launched the FBI investigation into UFOs in the country.

SITE OF ALIEN LORE

WHAT: The birth of UFOs in the US

WHERE: The Winthrop Hotel and the Tacoma Waterfront

COST: Free

PRO TIP: Every year in June, the Men in Black Festival takes place near Tacoma and celebrates the Maury Island incident.

UFO mural in Des Moines

CHAMBERS BAY TUNNELS

Were the post-apocalyptic structures by a golf course used to build Seattle?

Chambers Bay Gravel Quarry
Photo courtesy of Tacoma Public Library

Did you know that Washington's Chambers Bay Golf Course both hosted the US Open and features post-apocalyptic concrete buildings that date back to the 1890s? The skeletal structures that linger across the golf course have inspired indie films, photo sessions, and even the nesting decisions of local osprey. Their original construction was foundational to the history of Tacoma.

In 1890, the Pacific Bridge Company got the contract to provide gravel from what is now Chambers Bay to the US military for the construction of Fort Casey, Fort Flagger, and Fort Warden on Puget Sound. The remnants of the structures now on the golf course were part of the infrastructure used there to sort and mine the gravel. Those facilities had a conveyor belt that would take that gravel out, put it on a barge, and

---

The Steilacoom tribe traditionally occupied the Chambers Bay area because it was on a major trade route and was very close to Chambers Creek, which had magnificent salmon runs.

ship it up Puget Sound for use. When you explore these structures, you may see long yawning tunnels that extend underground. These were used as part of the conveyor system that moved gravel out and away. At its peak, the gravel quarry also had a long aerial wire that could move a scoop from one end of the quarry to the other.

The gravel itself was left after a massive glacier dragged itself across the area during the last ice age. This glacial movement formed most of the Puget Sound and left behind many gravel deposits. These gravel deposits are particularly hard and work really well for concrete construction. Not only were those three military forts built using Chambers Bay gravel but a vast majority of Seattle was also built with it. If you're ever out running at Chambers Bay or playing golf, you will know what those strange concrete structures are. That kind of rocks.

HISTORY-RICH GOLF COURSE

WHAT: A gravel quarry turned golf course

WHERE: 6320 Grandview Dr. W, University Place

COST: Free to run

PRO TIP: Take a kite on a windy day. The open field by Chambers Bay has excellent conditions for flying kites near Tacoma.

STADIUM HIGH SCHOOL

What is the story of America's Hogwarts?

It may look like an enchanted castle, but it is actually a public high school. Stadium High School has captured the imagination of the world for more than 100 years. It was meant to be a luxury hotel, but a financial crisis led to it being opened as a public school instead. It has been the set of several movies, including, most famously, *10 Things I Hate About You*, which came out in 1999.

It was built in 1891 by the Northern Pacific Railroad. Unfortunately, due to an unforeseen financial crisis in 1893, the railroad was forced to shutter the project and the building was left empty.

The structure was marked by a fire that destroyed some of the interior in October 1898. In 1904, the Tacoma School District

THE SCHOOL FROM *10 THINGS I HATE ABOUT YOU*

WHAT: The most beautiful public school in America

WHERE: 111 N E St.

COST: Fee to take a tour with Pretty Gritty Tours

PRO TIP: The original illustration that Hewitt and Hewitt gave to the railroad to pitch the design still hangs inside the office.

made the shrewd decision to make an offer on the abandoned castle and bought it for next to nothing, opening it for the first time two years later as a public high school, which it has remained.

Stadium High School has four floors, three basements, and four attic levels for a total of 11 levels. The architect got the district to buy the neighboring gulch and convert it into a massive amphitheater.

The Stadium became the public amphitheater of Tacoma, designed to have a seating capacity of 31,000 people. The most ever recorded was 64,000 people in attendance to see Theodore Roosevelt. The basement is a wonder. It contains several steam pipe tunnels and corridors from when it was built as a hotel. The original building even had a subterranean dog kennel and wine cellar, both of which have been sealed for obvious reasons.

The brick on the exterior of Stadium High was custom-ordered Roman brick. It was meant to be built with an ombre color pattern, but the workers didn't do that, and the brick is a calico pattern of colors.

RUST MANSION

TACOMA'S ICONIC MANSION

WHAT: The White House of the West

WHERE: 1001 N I St.

COST: Expensive to buy as a private home

PRO TIP: This is still a private residence, so please be respectful, but it is a killer location to go trick or treating.

What is the history of the White House of the West?

William Rust was one of the wealthiest citizens of Tacoma and the man responsible for expanding the Tacoma Smelter and Refining Company, which would later go on to be sold to ASARCO. The copper smelting facility was located along Ruston Way, and the company town built for its workers was called Smelterville until the citizens renamed it Ruston. Now it sits next to Tacoma to the north.

Rust was as wealthy as they come now that he had made a vast fortune with his smelting operation, and he needed a mansion to match his new status as a Tacoma elite. The 11,000-square-foot mansion was built for a staggering price of $220,000 in 1905. That would be almost $8 million today. Famous architect Ambrose Russel designed the mansion, affectionately known today as the White House of the West. The grand design, ballroom, and marble fireplaces were famous in their own right, but in 1911 the Rust Mansion became infamous. Rust's eldest son, Howard, died suddenly from a heart attack just days before his 25th birthday. Rust and his wife were so distraught that they sold the Rust Mansion for a fraction of

The second Rust Mansion was built nearby at 521 North Yakima.

what they spent on it and moved a few blocks away to another mansion they had built.

The official account is that Howard Rust had an artery rupture while he was at a ranch in eastern Washington. Rumors have long been circulated that his death was more nefarious, that perhaps Howard killed himself or was murdered. There's no evidence that's been discovered to back that up, though, just the strange silence of the Rust family. After Howard died, they never spoke of it publicly.

The dark stories and legends of curses have lingered in the halls and lavish rooms of the Rust Mansion to this day.

HOSMER HOUSE

What is Tacoma's oldest home?

Officially Tacoma's oldest residence, this bright yellow home was built in 1875. However, it wasn't always located where it is currently. It used to be up the street at 750 St. Helens Avenue, facing out toward the water.

When Theodore Hosmer moved to Tacoma, he quickly became the most important person in town. Hosmer was the agent for the Tacoma Land Co. in charge of parceling off and selling the newly acquired railroad holdings that would become the city of Tacoma. The railroad's main office and Tacoma's city hall were both built directly next to the Hosmer home. Within a year, Hosmer's wife, Louise, got very sick, and they moved back to Philadelphia. As soon as the Hosmers left, the house lost its clout and became a boardinghouse to help accommodate the population boom that was exploding into Tacoma.

Now that it no longer belonged to the most important man in town, it was just a lowly boardinghouse. The city wanted it away from the main street. In 1904 it was lifted and moved down the street and turned 90 degrees so that it faced the new Theater District. From there it continued to serve as a boardinghouse, even after Henry Rhodes, owner of the Rhodes department store, bought it and renamed it the Exley, after his dad's hometown.

Today it's an apartment building, with 12 rooms under the leadership of the Pioneer Human Services group. All around

---

The neighborhood around the Hosmer House has some of Tacoma's most interesting buildings, including the Bostwick Building. The Bostwick was opened in 1889 by Tacoma's first doctor, Henry Bostwick.

the Hosmer House, the city has expanded skyward in sharp lines of concrete and glass, but the Douglas fir home built in 1875 continues to welcome and shelter those who arrive to the City of Destiny. It stands sentinel against the strong tide of time and reminds us of the dream that first kindled Tacoma into a city.

OLDEST HOME IN TOWN

WHAT: Tacoma's oldest house

WHERE: 309 S 9th St.

COST: Free to look at

PRO TIP: You can get a great view of Tacoma's historic home by visiting one of the many historic theaters on 9th Street.

BUFFALO SOLDIERS MUSEUM

Who were the Buffalo Soldiers?

There are only two dedicated museums in the US that tell the story of the Buffalo Soldiers. One in Houston, the other here in Tacoma. The museum holds a diverse and intense look at the contributions soldiers of color have made to the US armed forces.

After the Civil War, in 1866, Congress passed legislation to create six all–African American army units. The Buffalo Soldiers Museum says, "The units were identified as the 9th and 10th cavalry and the 38th, 39th, 40th, and 41st infantry regiments. In 1869, the four infantry regiments were reorganized to form the 24th and 25th infantry regiments." These men served the US military with distinction. The name Buffalo Soldiers came from the fact that an estimated 20 percent of cavalry members were black soldiers during the wars that expanded west, commonly called the Indian Wars. Buffalo Soldiers was a name popularized by the Cheyenne and other Plains Indians, who saw a resemblance between the dark, curly hair of these service members of color and the hair on buffalo.

Buffalo soldiers were integral in military training like the American Lake Maneuvers that took place in 1904. Along the banks of nearby American Lake, military units from the

AN UNEXPECTED HISTORY STOP

WHAT: A museum dedicated to preserving and sharing the legacy of America's all-black military units

WHERE: 1940 S Wilkeson St.

COST: Donations encouraged

PRO TIP: You can also visit the American Lake Maneuvers heritage area down by Lakewood.

US Army and the National Guard conducted maneuvers and mock skirmishes to prepare for combat. There were more than 4,000 Buffalo Soldiers present for these war games, and they were instrumental in proving the value of the region as a training ground for military preparation. This area later became Joint Base Lewis–McChord.

The director of the Buffalo Soldiers Museum is Jackie Jones-Hook. Her father, William Jones, was a Buffalo Soldier. His dying wish was that his time as a Buffalo Soldier would be preserved for future generations. Jackie made good on her promise to her father, and in 2012 the museum opened. There is a collection of items like blankets, saddles, and letters from Buffalo Soldiers that lived in the region.

You can find a great exhibit on the American Lake Maneuvers at the DuPont Historical Museum.

THE PROCTOR CLOCK

Can a clock remind us of love?

There is a stunning clock in the Proctor Neighborhood that was built by a local gentleman named Edward "Doc" Farrens. Doc had been in Tacoma for more than four decades and loved clocks with a deep passion. He was an avid collector, with clocks he had picked up in Algiers, India, New York, San Francisco, and London. The London ones had some special meaning for him because Doc had helped with the restoration of Big Ben in London after WWII.

Doc took his knowledge of clocks and love of mechanics and worked on the biggest timepieces in Tacoma. The clocks of Old City Hall, Lincoln High School, and the clock tower on Bridgeport Way were all repaired by Doc at some point.

One of his most iconic projects was to design and build from scratch the clock that stands along Proctor Street today. Doc and his wife, Elsie, used to eat together all the time in the Proctor Neighborhood, and this street had one of their favorite restaurants. After Elsie passed away, Doc made a clock as a memorial for her and a tribute to their time together. In 1999, he built the $45,000 timepiece that was paid for primarily by the North End Neighborhood Council. The clock was erected on the junction of North 27th Street and North Proctor Street, in front of Doc and Elsie's favorite restaurant.

Street clocks were a necessity in early Tacoma, when not everyone had a watch, because they let people know when the streetcars would be arriving.

HANDMADE CLOCK IN PROCTOR

WHAT: A custom timepiece made with love

WHERE: 2702 N Proctor St.

COST: Free

PRO TIP: Doc and Elsie's old restaurant is gone, but if you've got time you should check out any of the wonderful eateries in Proctor right by the clock today.

Doc had to get creative with several of the parts, and those that he couldn't find he machined himself. The clock has a 70-pound pendulum and a massive brass eagle with a three-foot wingspan perched on top. The clock was built with a deep knowledge gathered over a lifetime and set up for the one woman who made Doc feel like he had all the time in the world.

JACK THE BEAR

Did a Tacoma hotel adopt a beer-drinking bear?

Photo courtesy of Tacoma News Tribune

In the late 1800s, one of the most beautiful structures in Tacoma was the grand Tacoma Hotel.

The hotel received an unexpected mascot one day when an abandoned black bear cub was adopted by the hotel staff after a drunken logger had abducted it from the woods. The logger was discontent that the bear would not perform on command and threatened to beat it until the hotel staff took the bear and affectionately named him Jack.

The hotel staff built Jack a little enclosure in the back garden, where he lived.

One of the most iconic things about Jack was that he would walk into the hotel bar, where the barkeep poured a stein of beer for Jack. Jack would hook it with his claws and kick it back. Yes, Jack the black bear could drink a beer.

Over the years, the Tacoma Police Department has received calls from people who believed they had seen a black bear wandering through Firefighter's Park.

A TRIBUTE TO A BEER-DRINKING BEAR

WHAT: A mural depicting Jack, the famous black bear

WHERE: Below the 11th Street Bridge

COST: Free

PRO TIP: If you go to see the mural, you will see a painted likeness of Jack the bear hidden on the foot of the bridge.

Everything seemed like it was going to be okay until one fateful day when a rookie cop mistook Jack for a wild bear and opened fire. He killed Jack with a single shot, and then he realized the error he had made. The police station decided that it would be a waste to let Jack's sacrifice go without a celebration, so they had a barbecue where Jack was the main course. Then they paid to have what was left of Jack stuffed by a local taxidermist and gave him back to the hotel. Jack remained in the main lobby of the Tacoma Hotel from 1884 until 1892, before moving to the Ferry Museum. In 1958, Jack's taxidermy remains were loaned to Mrs. Everett Grigg II, but from there the trail goes cold. Is Jack out there today, thirsty and watching over the city? We can only hope so.

MASON'S MUMMY

AN EGYPTIAN HIGH PRIEST

WHAT: Tacoma's resident mummified Egyptian priest

WHERE: The deep vaults of the Washington State Historical Society

COST: Free

PRO TIP: You can see the scans, busts, reconstructions, and more of Ankh-Wennefer and his family online at the historical society's digital collection.

Did one of Tacoma's most prominent businessmen abduct a high priest from Egypt?

Allen C. Mason is one of Tacoma's greatest patrons and boosters. He was a wealthy real estate developer who made a fortune selling plots in Tacoma. One of his greatest contributions was a marketing tool, the "Star of Destiny." Mason had a graphic made of a

Photo courtesy of Washington State Historical Society

star with the word "Tacoma" printed boldly in the center with beams of light radiating outward. Each beam of light had text recommending the newly developed city, like "No poisonous bugs nor reptiles!" Mason ran this ad in papers all through the East Coast, and it worked. People came to Tacoma in droves to buy homes and lots from Mason.

On a trip around the world, Mason bought the 2,500-year-old mummified remains of a priest named Ankh-Wennefer, and Mason had them shipped back to Tacoma, where in 1891 he held an "unwrapping party" at his office. Mason kept Ankh-Wennefer in his office with him until 1897, when he donated the mummy to the Ferry Museum, which would later become the Washington State Historical Society Research Center.

Anhk-Wennefer was on display from 1959 to 1983. Many of Tacoma's students went to visit the Egyptian priest at some point. The mummified remains went on their last voyage in public to the Kelowna Museums in British Columbia in 1993. From there, he went underground at the Washington State Historical Society Research Center.

In the early 2000s, scans were made of Ankh-Wennefer's remains and coffins. There is a rich exhibit online of what he looked like when he was alive and what his life may have been like. For now, though, it seems the dark vaults of Tacoma will hold him as he continues to rest in the ornate sarcophagus. The Historical Society has chosen to no longer display Ankh-Wennefer's remains out of respect for the dead.

The Washington State Historical Society building is a treasure trove of state historic relics, with a series of mysterious and secure rooms that all are climate controlled.

REBECCA CARR

TACOMA'S PSYCHIC

WHAT: Home of Tacoma's most famous clairvoyant

WHERE: The site of the current Tacoma Mountaineers, 2302 N 30th St.

COST: Free

PRO TIP: If you walk down the street toward the water, you will find a little-known marker that denotes the location of Job Carr's original cabin alongside the train tracks. There is a replica of Job's cabin just down 30th Street nearby that was built in the early 2000s and houses a museum of early Tacoma and the Carr family.

Was Tacoma once home to the state's most famous psychic?

Rebecca Carr was affectionately known as the "Witch of Old Town," or "Mother Staley." She was a spiritualist who grew up on the East Coast and eventually married her sweetheart, Job Carr. Job would later go on to be the founder of Old Town Tacoma, but by that point, he and Rebecca had been divorced for some time.

Her main claim to fame in Tacoma was that she had the reputation of being a clairvoyant. It was well known throughout the region that if you handed her something you had carried with you on your person, Rebecca would be able to see through the murky veil of time and get a clear picture of the future that was about to unfold for you.

There are several accounts of her accurately predicting the future of Tacoma, but it is the personal accounts that leave the most profound impact. Frank W. Sullivan, a business leader in the Tacoma area, went to Rebecca to ask about his fiancée. He handed Rebecca a handkerchief, and she calmly said that she saw a heavyset dark man arriving on a train and embracing Frank's fiancée. He said that he had no affiliation with the train and that that couldn't be about him, but then he recalled the handkerchief he was using was handed to him that morning by his fiancée on loan from her brother, who, you may have

Photo courtesy of Washington State Historical Society

guessed already, was, in fact, a darker heavyset man who worked as an engineer for the railroad. Sullivan then tried again with a pocketknife he had carried on him for some time, and Rebecca very clearly saw the future that unfolded before him.

Rebecca's witch shack, I mean cottage, was located in Old Town Tacoma, where the Tacoma Mountaineers club is today.

Old Town Tacoma was separate from New Tacoma until they were consolidated into just Tacoma in 1884.

SNAKE LAKE PARADISE

Is it a lake of snakes or one of the city's most precious wetlands?

Right in the urban heart of Tacoma is a 71-acre paradise that seems shielded from all of the noise and chaos around it. Snake Lake began as a recreational stop on a pleasure train that moved passengers from the crowded streets of downtown Tacoma to a resort on American Lake. Over the years, the enjoyment people found at Snake Lake reached the stuff of legend, and more and more people started going there in the summer to enjoy nature and in the winter to ice-skate on the frozen surface.

Snake Lake is easily overlooked as it is hidden right in the heart of a major neighborhood and runs below a highway. Despite being in the center of it all, it feels like you are in a remote forest once you enter the trails. It always had a reputation as a peaceful and pastoral setting in the busy city center, but in the 1970s there was a plan to take state Highway 16 right through it.

Eventually, a plan was made to preserve the wetland by bridging the state highway right over the top of the lake and leaving the wetland as untouched as possible. The bridge is at such a height that it doesn't interfere with drainage or the nature below. Today, when you explore Snake Lake, it feels like you have been transported to a different land entirely. When you walk along the lakeshore, it's difficult to know that you're within a city at all.

HIDDEN NATURE SANCTUARY

WHAT: A protected urban wetland

WHERE: 1919 S Tyler St.

COST: Free

PRO TIP: Check out their website to see the various camps and educational programs that are operated out at the Nature Center year-round.

Today Snake Lake and the Tacoma Nature Center are refuges for a variety of animals, a protected wetland, and an educational center for people to learn more about ways to interact with and preserve nature throughout the region. The staff and buildings on-site are dedicated to informing young generations about the importance of maintaining wetlands, especially in urban environments.

As for the name, it comes from the fact that in the earliest days of the lake, the shores would swarm with garter snakes drawn to the bounty throughout the area.

POINT DEFIANCE

Is Tacoma's largest park an old-growth forest?

The northernmost point of Tacoma has been reserved for natural wonder. Point Defiance Park is a 720-plus-acre old-growth forest park. Originally, the area was an old-growth forest that got tapped by the US military when they thought that they might need to put in a military installation in preparation for a conflict with Spain. The Spanish–American War, however, played out mostly in Cuba and the Philippines, and so there was no need to have a stronghold built in Puget Sound.

Thus, the US military never developed a fort in Point Defiance, and it was turned over to the City of Tacoma as part of a park system when President Grover Cleveland signed a bill in 1888.

The boathouse, rose garden, and zoo were the first additions to this new park. "Zoo" is a very relative term for a slightly fenced field for elk to run in and a pit for bears. Some of the most famous bear stories of Tacoma come from this time.

TACOMA'S LARGEST PARK

WHAT: More than 720 acres of old-growth forest and city park

WHERE: 5400 N Pearl St.

COST: Free

PRO TIP: Check the calendar of events to see what is happening at Fort Nisqually. When you stop in, be sure to greet the resident fort cats that meet and greet the guests.

Another interesting addition was the Nereides Baths, Tacoma's first indoor pool. A building was constructed in 1906 to house a pool filled with water from Puget Sound that was pumped in and heated to 80 degrees for year-round swimming. The pool and building were removed in the 1930s, but Point Defiance got one of its best features then. Fort Nisqually was the first European settlement in the area. Originally located in DuPont, two of the buildings for the original fort were disassembled and brought up to Tacoma by the Works Progress Administration. It is now the Fort Nisqually Living History Museum and welcomes visitors all year.

With miles upon miles of walking trails, beautiful coastline, and several opportunities for education, Point Defiance is one of the most treasured and beloved parts of Tacoma.

Point Defiance's first "zoo" didn't have just elk, deer, and bears, it also hosted a monkey.

SALISHAN'S FORGOTTEN CITY

Are the remains of a forgotten city in the woods by Tacoma?

Tacoma has had a long working relationship with the US military. During the 1940s there was an effort to make sure housing was available for all the enlisted servicemen arriving to deploy from Fort Lewis. The Salishan neighborhood was created for these individuals, which later became a low-income housing area. First known as the Portland Avenue Defense Housing Project, the name was later changed to Salishan at the suggestion of University of Puget Sound librarian Warren Perry. Salishan refers to the language family of the Coast Salish peoples.

The area was cleared to make way for 2,000 rapidly constructed homes and 6,500-plus residents. Some of the homes were designed to be temporary, so at the conclusion of World War II, 400 of the houses were demolished. The remainder were converted to low-income housing in the early 1950s.

Where the homes were destroyed, the area was left open. The streets that had connected them and the sidewalks and power poles all lingered as a reminder of what had been there. The Tacoma police used to use the empty streets for defensive-driving and simulated-firearms training.

This empty neighborhood was considered for a golf course or a city dump, but the plans were all rejected.

When you visit today, you can explore the abandoned remains of a neighborhood that was erased from the map, leaving only streets and sidewalks behind to tell the tale.

The final plan that stuck was to convert the area into part of Swan Creek Park. Swan Creek is a greenbelt with a wonderful creek that runs through. There is some debate as to where the name came from. One of the earliest residents of the area was a Puyallup man named John Swan. Of course, the Puyallup name for the area is *Bəsx^{w} uqid* in Lushootseed, which means "a place that has swans." No one seems to know if the park is named after the creek or the man.

NEIGHBORHOOD TURNED INTO PARK

WHAT: The remains of a neighborhood, long forgotten

WHERE: 2106 E 44th St.

COST: Free

PRO TIP: Bring some boots and explore Swan Creek nearby as well.

PUGET GULCH PARK

Can you turn a dangerous gulch into a nice city park?

The City of Tacoma has a great many gulches that run through it. These are long geographical features that can sometimes extend more than a mile and are often 200 feet deep. They proved to be an issue for early Tacoma because they were so steep and deep that they couldn't easily be filled in or developed.

Puget Gulch was first donated in 1888 by Allen C. Mason, but it was made famous in 1891 when some locals found trace amounts of gold in the creek at the bottom. Many excited prospectors came to the gulch, but the gold never panned out. Then the gulch became a dark and undesirable place. Invasive ivy and local blackberries choked out the other plants and blocked out the light. As the gulch continued to be used for industrial and municipal waste drainage, it grew worse. A seedy element took root in the gulch and people began to avoid it. By 2000, a volunteer group with the nonprofit Puget Creek Restoration Society was formed, and together with Metro Parks they worked to restore Puget Gulch.

Tacoma has more than 15 historic gulches, but two of the best to explore are Puget Gulch and Julia's Gulch.

Inside the gulch, you'll find a variety of secret sculptures and hints as to the history of the region and the usage of the gulch today. One of the most obvious is the massive salmon. This was one of hundreds of fiberglass salmon called the Soul Salmon, made as part of an early 2000s effort to bring awareness to the environmental issues harming salmon. This one must have worked because hundreds of hours have gone into restoring, cleaning, and helping the gulch. With the construction of a fish passage, the final step fell into place and now salmon have returned to spawn up the creek.

TRASH PATCH TURNED INTO TREASURED PARK

WHAT: A hidden stone with the story of the watershed

WHERE: Near the lower end of Puget Gulch Park

COST: Free

PRO TIP: Park at the top near the playground and take the stunning walk down into the gulch or park near the bottom, and your return journey to the car will all be downhill.

HADDAWAY HALL

What is that massive mansion on the edge of Tacoma all about?

A MANSION FIT FOR ROYALTY

WHAT: Lavish former home of a prominent family

WHERE: 4301 N Stevens St.

COST: Depends on the market

PRO TIP: The home is still a private residence, but it will occasionally be on the Historic Homes of Tacoma Tour, which will get you inside.

The Weyerhaeuser timber family has long been one of the largest private landowners in North America. After accepting their timber claim in the 1800s, they moved their headquarters to Tacoma in 1900 and began the operation of turning trees into money after purchasing 900,000 acres from the Northern Pacific Railroad. John Weyerhaeuser and his wife, Anna, arrived by 1915 and had their Jacobean mansion built by 1923. A traditionally German and understated family, the Weyerhaeusers, though incredibly wealthy, never took it upon themselves to flaunt that wealth outward. However, John was swayed by his strong-willed wife. She wanted to have the largest and grandest mansion in the Pacific Northwest. He politely dismissed the request, but she had him build it anyhow. He affectionately called it Haddaway Hall because "once again she had her way."

The Weyerhaeusers owned many buildings in Tacoma, but one of the most famous was the home that George H. Weyerhaeuser was living at when he was kidnapped at age 9. It's located at 410 North 4th Street.

Photo courtesy of Tacoma Public Library

The Weyerhaeusers lived there until their deaths in the 1930s, and then for a time it served as a home for the Sisters of St. Dominic. When the nuns left, it became a private home again.

There are a multitude of secret passages, hidden cupboards, and even a walk-in silver safe in the plating room. Those few who have been invited inside have celebrated the acclaimed pipe organ in the drawing room. The organ sits humbly in the corner of the room while a mess of vacuum pipes lurks in the basement below. Secret panels abound, even a hidden iron gate that could unfold from a concealed pocket to separate the servants' quarters from the main family wing.

ELKS TEMPLE

Why does Tacoma have its own Spanish Steps?

Originally built in 1916, the benevolent protective order of Elks Lodge was a beautiful part of downtown Tacoma. It was the official Elks order for generations until the 1970s, when the Elks got priced out of the building due to declining membership. In the days before federal social security, clubs like the Elks and the Eagles offered financial security for workplace injuries and help for families if a member died.

For years, the Elks hosted meetings and balls inside the building. One of the most interesting features of the structure is the Spanish Steps. The architect, Édouard Champney, designed the building's fire escape to be a replica of the Spanish Steps in Rome. It's one of the most photographed parts of Tacoma now.

When the Elks officially left the building, it was sold to a man who would rent it to almost anyone. The building became an incubator for cultural events and a refuge for groups that hadn't had a place before. This grand

RESTAURANT AND HOTEL WITH TONS OF HISTORY

WHAT: A former Elks Club turned into an amazing event space for Tacoma

WHERE: 565 Broadway

COST: Price varies

PRO TIP: Pay attention to all the murals inside. They picture amazing parts of Tacoma's history, like the birth of noir and the UFOs that visited in the 1940s.

The basement of the former Elks building is a tiki lounge today, but it used to be a swimming pool. You can see historic photos of the pool on the wall outside the restaurant.

space had once been reserved for a very elite group of men and was now used for formal dances and events in the black community and even served as a formal meeting space for the gay community.

When the owner of the building passed away in 1986, the doors were sealed shut, and the empty interior became a proving ground for several of Tacoma's graffiti artists. Then after being empty for decades, it opened again in 2019. The McMenamin brothers, who are famous for converting historic properties into multiuse hotel and event spaces, bought the building and gave it new life.

Inside the former Elks building, you can now find a 40-room hotel, a brewery, a music venue, multiple bars and restaurants, and even a secret passageway to an underground bar.

FRISKO FREEZE

How did Tacoma's oldest drive-through restaurant get its name?

Frisko Freeze opened in 1950 and has long been considered Tacoma's first drive-through restaurant. It was immediately popular when Perry Smith opened this burger joint and has stayed popular. One of the true points of beauty for Frisko Freeze is the iconic sign, designed by a local neon sign company called Cliff Sign. They wanted it to be a beacon for the neighborhood, but no one could have guessed how successful and long-lasting their sign would be. It's a style of architecture called Googie, actually. Googie architecture is mid-century modern but was supposed to represent space-age futurism. Frisko Freeze is one of the few examples of this style in Tacoma.

Frisko Freeze had intended to open as an ice cream joint called Cream Freeze, with an emphasis on soft-serve ice cream, but Smith wanted to diversify his product and wasn't in love with the name. He and his wife, Roberta, went through a few different options, but he found his inspiration while listening to the Seattle Rainiers vs. the San Francisco Seals baseball game on the radio. Sports commentator Leo Lassen called the away team "the boys from Frisco" and Smith was hooked. He changed the name of his new restaurant to Frisko Freeze, and the rest was history.

Smith would operate Frisko Freeze for 40 years until his death in 1990. The Freeze was open 365 days a year with half days on Thanksgiving and Christmas. The Smiths created their own recipes and made everything from scratch. This,

---

After 70 years in business, Frisko Freeze still offers the burgers and milkshakes that made them famous from the start.

coupled with their involvement in the community, is what made Frisko Freeze legendary. Smith hired young men in the community, many of them working their first job. Some went on to great roles, such as the governorship for Booth Gardner, such a fan of Frisko Freeze that he kept a framed picture of the restaurant on his wall in his Olympia office.

TACOMA'S BURGER JOINT

WHAT: Tacoma's first drive-through restaurant

WHERE: 1201 Division Ave.

COST: Prices vary

PRO TIP: There are a lot of opinions here, but for this author, it doesn't get better than the blackberry shake.

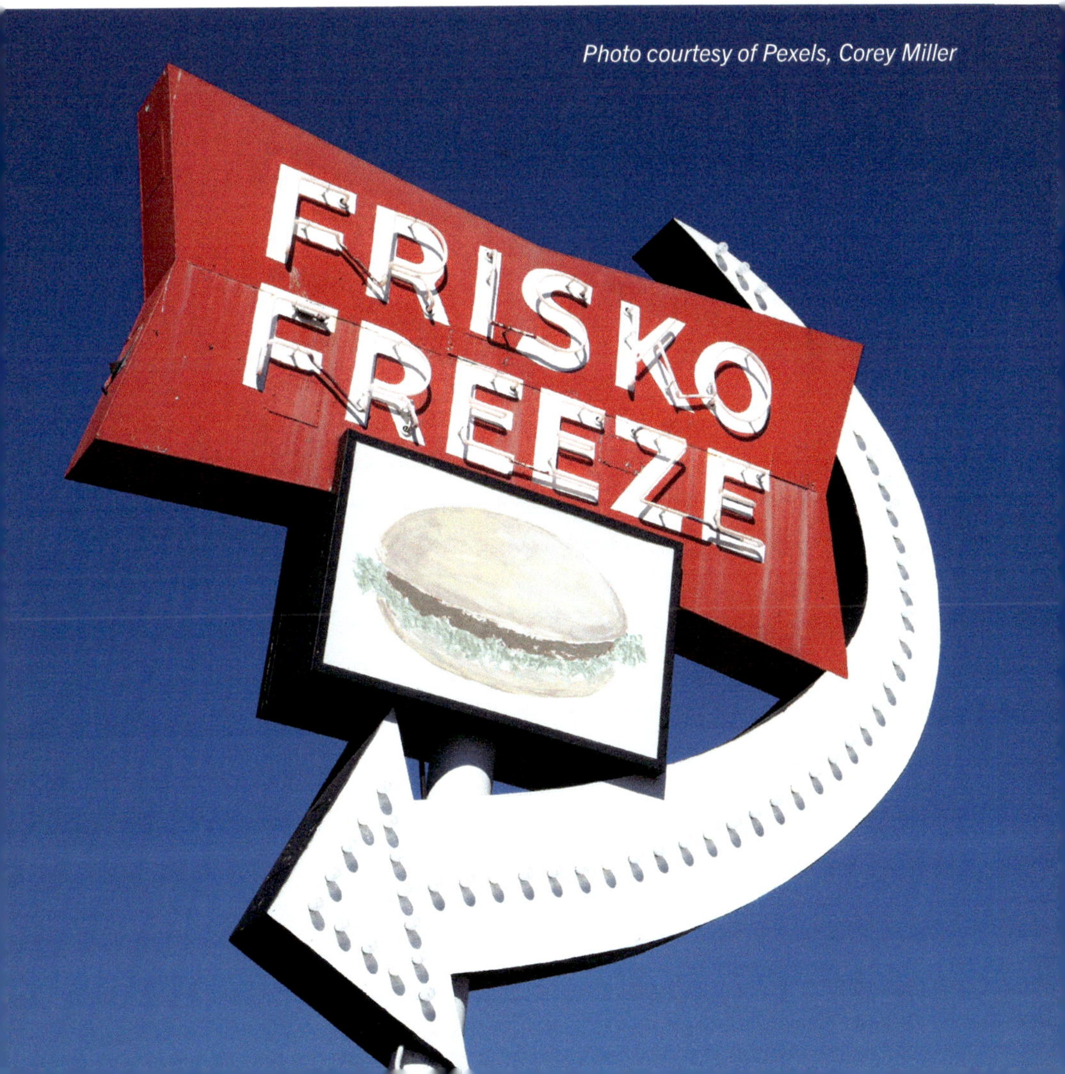

Photo courtesy of Pexels, Corey Miller

PRAIRIE LINE TRAIL

How do you make a skid row safe again?

As late as 1993, trains could be seen crossing Pacific Avenue, leaving the main line and jetting up into what was once the warehouse district of downtown Tacoma. As a bustling part-time community, it was essential to bridge the connection between water and rails, or as it was affectionately known, "where rails meet sales." The main line could be departed from onto a spur line known as the Prairie Line. The Prairie Line came up through the main brick buildings of our downtown warehouse district and connected the grocers, the paper company, the candy companies, and, most essentially, the breweries.

At the end of the Prairie Line was the Heidelberg Brewery Building, which was also Columbia Brewing at one point and is today the 7 Seas Brewery. This was a major artery of commerce for decades. By the 1970s, though, the Prairie Line fell into disuse and became something of a skid row in downtown Tacoma. Then, in the early 2000s, it was refurbished to a beautiful new use by the University of Washington Tacoma. Part of the rehabilitation of the historic line was to stud the whole path with interpretive art to help tell the story of Tacoma.

Today this interpretive trail is in fact along the original train line that connected the great country, but trains no longer whiz past. Much less dangerous, it is merely the track that transports you through time.

All along the Prairie Line Trail you'll see painted advertisements on the brick walls. These are historic ghost signs that were painted from the 1890s to the 1940s and are still there today.

THE PRAIRIE LINE

WHAT: An interpretive art trail on a former rail line

WHERE: 1900 Commerce St.

COST: Free

PRO TIP: Check out the online map at prairielinetrail.org and see info about all the art along the way.

MASONRY OWL

WHAT: The final works of stone made by Tacoma's last great mason

WHERE: The rear entrance to Anderson/Langdon Hall on University of Puget Sound's campus

COST: Free to visit, a bit more to attend

PRO TIP: The University of Puget Sound's current campus was developed starting in the 1920s and was designed to reflect the class and elegance of an English college. It has the charm of an old-world campus and makes for a wonderful park.

THE LAST STONE OWL

What did Tacoma's last great mason carve?

The railroad town of Tacoma was always looking for good resources. One of the best was the vein of sandstone south of Tacoma in the town of Wilkeson. It is easy to carve but less porous than other sandstone. In fact, according to W. P. Bonney's *History of Pierce County*, published in 1927, Wilkeson sandstone was recognized by the US government to be the only sandstone that didn't require additional waterproofing.

The first official building to be built in Tacoma with this special stone was St. Luke's Memorial Church. The last known, hand-carved piece of masonry, though, is a small owl that has gone overlooked for the last several decades.

A local enterprise known as the Walker Cut Stone Company was responsible for hiring and deploying many of the masons who created decorative stonework for Tacoma's many buildings. The main masonry building originally operated off Center Street. It was a hub for stonemasons in Tacoma, and many of our historic structures bear decorative stone to this day that was once hand-carved by skilled craftsmen here in the city.

Lloyd Livernash was the last living carver from the Walker Cut Stone Company, and his final work was to create a pair of hand-carved stone owls for the doorway on the University of Puget Sound campus. These two owls keep watch over the eastern entrance to Anderson/Langdon Hall. While Tacoma has continued to develop and evolve over the years, the skilled stonework that was foundational to it has remained. These owls are the last line in a chapter of Tacoma's history that was written in stone. Livernash, the last of the great stone masons in Tacoma, passed away in 2021.

The Wilkeson Sandstone Quarry no longer sells stone, but you can drive out to see it and explore the small town of Wilkeson nearby.

O'NEIL CAST IRON MUSEUM

Does Tacoma have one of the best-stocked cast-iron museums in the world?

In 1957, Larry O'Neil married his high school sweetheart, Marg, and the couple needed a solid piece of cookware for their new life. Larry bought a cast-iron pan and brought it home. He loved it. Marg loved it. Together they invested in a few more cast-iron items: pans, bakeware, ovens, skillets, and more. What started as a whim slowly heated up into an obsession, and today the O'Neils run the nation's largest cast-iron museum from their private home in Tacoma. With more than 13,000 pieces of cast-iron cookware, they have curated a collection that spans hundreds of years.

It's difficult to know when it developed into the large collection that it is today, but what's for sure is that the massive assortment of cast iron is unrivaled. The O'Neils have an entire wall of decorative trivets. They have sturdy items like well-used Dutch

ONE-OF-A-KIND COLLECTION

WHAT: The nation's largest collection of curated cast iron

WHERE: Edge of Tacoma

COST: Free to visit

PRO TIP: Tours can be arranged by reaching out to the duo. Email them at loneil7701@aol.com to arrange a visit or go to their Instagram @oneilfamilycastiron.

If you love niche collections, consider a visit to the LeMay Collection at Marymount. They have a room of just vintage radios, among other treasurers.

Photo courtesy of Edsel Little, Wikimedia Commons

ovens as well as lesser-known trinkets like utensils and enameled cookware. There was never a plan, just a deep love for the craft.

Today the couple runs their collection out of an enormous barn on their property on the outskirts of Tacoma. They offer buying, selling, and trading, so if you ever find yourself enchanted by the idea of cast iron, this is the place for you.

THE ELEPHANT HOUSE

Was there a collection of more than 3,000 elephants in Tacoma?

Ray Gamble was one of the most eccentric individuals to ever arrive on the shores of the City of Destiny. Gamble had arrived in Tacoma in the 1890s. He was almost broke and worked odd jobs. While here, he invented a fine sawdust mixture and the process to create it. He designed it as a way to control the smell of fish but made millions when he sold the idea to the US military and DuPont. The cellulose buffer also worked as an excellent accelerant and stabilizer. It was a great way to simultaneously make dynamite safer and more explosive. With his new millions Gamble could focus on his true passions, magic and elephants.

In 1939, Gamble bought the former 1921 Robert Walker mansion and converted it into his private home. He added a stage in the basement for magic shows and several hidden panels and compartments to make the home even more mysterious

Photo courtesy of Tacoma Public Library

and enchanting. The house was considered one of the finest party spots in all of Tacoma, with Gamble's parties being the stuff of legend. He hosted many famous visitors over the years, including Orson Welles, General Douglas MacArthur, Will Rogers, and even Harry Houdini's widow, Beatrice.

The home earned its name over the years because Gamble didn't just collect high profile friends and magic tricks, he loved all things elephant. He had a collection of elephant figures numbering more than 3,000, considered the world's largest. He kept ruby-encrusted elephants carved from ivory on the same shelf as small 10-cent plastic elephants. When Gamble passed away, his collection was sold, but several of the stone elephants, lamps, and statues remain at the elephant house today.

THE MAGICIAN'S HOME

WHAT: The home of a famous magician who made his fortune in explosives

WHERE: 3411 N 30th St.

COST: Free to look, but it is a private residence

PRO TIP: Ray Gamble left a collection of elephant statues outside the home, and today the current resident is a local artist who often has fiberglass statues out front.

Photo courtesy of Tacoma Public Library

Ray Gamble invested in many buildings in Tacoma, and one, the Casablanca Apartments, still has a lot of the wacky art he decorated it with from his travels around the world. The basement has a whole collection of his touches.

THE CHANGER

Where does Tacoma's most powerful and ancient rock lie buried and forgotten?

The Puyallup Tribe have lived in the area we know as Tacoma since time immemorial. When the US advanced westward and claimed territory in the region with the Treaty of Medicine Creek and the subsequent Puget Sound Treaty Wars, many of the significant cultural artifacts and markers of the Puyallup Tribe were lost in the conflict. One that has captured the imagination of many over the last 150 years is known as "The Changer."

Once located in the area known today as Firefighter's Park was a large stone decorated with the image of a man. Herbert Hunt describes it in his book *Tacoma: Its History and Its Builders*, "Prized among the Indians was a great rock . . . Its surface bore the figure of a man . . . The stone on the beach once had been a man. The Indians venerated it."

Photo courtesy of Tacoma Public Library

MISSING PETROGLYPH STONE

WHAT: A sacred rock with a petroglyph buried beneath the shore

WHERE: Half Moon Yard

COST: Free

PRO TIP: Go to the scenic overlook in Firefighter's Park to get the best view of where the stone used to be visible and is located today.

The surrounding area known as Half Moon Bay was a small bay at the base of the rapidly growing city of Tacoma. When it was filled in, it became Half Moon Yard, a switching yard for the railroad. Half Moon Yard continues to exist today, and hundreds of Union Pacific and BNSF trains carry millions of dollars worth of goods over it every day.

Today the sacred rock, The Changer, lies just beneath the surface. For years, there has been a belief that the careless act of destroying something so important and revered has brought bad luck on Tacoma, and only making amends and returning the stone can reverse this curse. Of course, the stone has been preserved against destruction by slumbering underground. It would be a terrible shame to lose the knowledge of it, though.

Several prominent historians in the region continue to maintain that simple ground-penetrating radar would be enough to locate the sacred rock, but there has never been enough interest or funding to make that a reality.

Another example of these ancient petroglyphs exists out on Bainbridge Island. A rock there has carvings thought to be 3,000 years old.

LOCAL SHIPWRECK

WHAT: Tacoma's cursed ship

WHERE: 180 feet down in Commencement Bay

COST: Free

PRO TIP: In the 1970s, a woman found a bottle on the beach of Acapulco, Mexico. It had been sealed with wax and inside was a letter from Robert Laughter from the *Andelana*. He had written it and thrown it overboard in Tacoma only for it to drift down the coast and wait in Mexico for 80 years to be discovered and returned to Tacoma.

ANDELANA

Does a cursed ship still haunt Tacoma with a lingering curse?

A 300-foot British cargo ship vanished into Tacoma's harbor and has never been recovered. The loss of the *Andelana* remains one of the worst maritime tragedies and one of the deepest mysteries of Tacoma.

On January 13, 1899, the *Andelana* was at anchor in Commencement Bay. Under command of Captain George Stalling, it had left Shanghai with a full cargo and unloaded its hold at Tacoma some months later. The crew had been spooked that the ship was cursed, and half of them quit upon arrival. A series of misfortunes had struck them on their journey around the world from England, and one of their sailors, a man named Robert Murdoch—or Robert Laughter, as he called himself—had just been detained by the captain and put into the Tacoma jail for allegedly abducting a child. The series of unfortunate events

> Multiple pieces of the *Andelana* continue to haunt the region, including a model of the ship carved from the wreckage of the 1900 streetcar disaster in Tacoma.

Crew of the Andelana. *Photo courtesy of Tacoma Public Library*

had the crew on edge, and Captain Stalling himself had a recurring nightmare that he was going to drown on the ship.

Stalling decided to hire local photographer Wilhelm Hester to come and take a photograph of the whole crew as a good luck totem. After the photo was taken, the *Andelana* vanished into the bay. Some local historians believe that a strong gale was responsible.

A diver in the area, William Baldwin, was brought in to try to recover the wreck. He found it immediately and set a world record for descending into 180 feet of water. On his second attempt, his pressurizing pump blew a seal, and as his suit depressurized, Baldwin died quickly under Commencement Bay.

All attempts to recover the ship have ended tragically. Today, the location of the *Andelana* is a mystery, and despite the technology getting better and better, this 300-foot iron-hulled ship remains elusive.

OLD WOMAN'S GULCH

What is beneath the Stadium Bowl?

When Stadium High School first opened, it was called Tacoma High School. Shortly after, it was renamed Stadium High School to celebrate one of the great achievements of the city thus far, turning a shanty town into a massive amphitheater. From the late 1890s on, the gulch that extended into North Tacoma became a refuge for women who were widowed due to seafaring or fishing accidents. Often, if a man died at sea, his widow would be left penniless and alone. Many of these women found solace and makeshift homes or shanties at the bottom of a gulch that became known as Old Woman's Gulch, certainly not flattering but descriptive of the community's feeling toward the place.

The team that finished construction of Stadium High School and opened it in 1906 wanted to turn the gulch into a playing field. It required them to sluice the sides of the gulch to flood dirt into the basin and level it

THE FORGOTTEN REFUGE

WHAT: A former refuge for widows, now a stadium

WHERE: 111 N E St.

COST: Free

PRO TIP: You can visit the stadium during special events and when school isn't in session.

The remains of Old Woman's Gulch are still buried at the bottom of the Stadium High field.

out. The sides of the gulch were steep, and the lowest portion of the gulch was often below the water during high tide. There was pushback from the women living in the gulch, but when the body of a disgruntled worker was found dead in a tree the community rallied together to "clean up the gulch."

Old Woman's Gulch was slated for destruction, and the widows were forced from their homes. One woman, whose name has sadly been lost to history, refused to leave. Herbert Hunt, in his book *Tacoma: Its History and Its Builders*, said, "Several small houses built by squatters stood in the gulch, and some of the occupants were removed with difficulty. One woman became hysterical and remained in her hut until the water, mud, and stones poured into her back door."

The Stadium went in and the shanty town was forgotten.

Photo courtesy of Tacoma Public Library

ENGINE HOUSE NO. 9

Is Tacoma's hottest restaurant in an old firehouse?

Tacoma has the distinction of being the first city in western Washington to have a professional full-time fire department. Up until the 1890s, most fire departments were volunteer organizations. But the dangerous fires that destroyed Seattle and Spokane in 1889 were enough cause for cities like Tacoma to take issue. Tacoma had established a volunteer fire department in 1880, but just two weeks after the Seattle fire of 1889 the city council voted to move the volunteer department to salary and made it the first professional full-time fire department in the state.

With this new professional team of firefighters, the city wanted to have some fires stations and engine houses to match. In the early 1900s, several brick firehouses were constructed throughout Tacoma. Many of them are still there today. A few, like Fire House No. 2 and Fire House No. 13, still operate as fire stations. Some have transitioned to other uses for their historic structure.

One of the best examples is Engine House No. 9, first constructed in 1907. It served as Tacoma's firehouse for decades.

Photo courtesy of Tacoma Public Library

It has the unique distinction of being the last engine house in Tacoma to have a fire engine that was drawn by horses. The fire horses—Nip, Dick, and Joe—retired in 1919. When the horses passed away, local legend says that they were buried in the back of the engine house, which eventually was paved over into an alley. The engine house closed in 1965.

In the 1970s, the building became the first microbrewery in Tacoma, and today it is still a restaurant, the E9 Firehouse. The back end of the restaurant was converted from the old stables, and the names of the fire horses are painted over their individual stalls to this day.

HISTORIC FIRE HOUSE

WHAT: An engine house converted into a hot restaurant

WHERE: 611 N Pine St.

COST: Price varies

PRO TIP: E9 Firehouse used to brew all their own beer in-house and then in the former fireplace store next door. They moved their brewery downtown by 2020 and operate their taproom in an old muffler shop. Today Engine House No. 9 is a restaurant and events space with no brewery inside.

The brass fire pole and several other functional elements of the firehouse still remain, though using the fire pole is discouraged.

BROWNS POINT LIGHTHOUSE

THE LIGHTHOUSE

WHAT: A former lighthouse keeper's cottage, the old lighthouse still in action

WHERE: 201 Tulalip St. NE, Browns Point

COST: Free to visit. Prices vary for the stay.

PRO TIP: The lighthouse is currently run by the US Coast Guard. The operation of the nation's lighthouses was done by a branch called the Bureau of Lighthouses from 1910 to 1939, when the US Coast Guard officially took over management of all domestic lighthouses and navigational aids.

Can you stay in a historic lighthouse cottage?

The iconic Art Deco lighthouse located at Browns Point is one of the most notable features of the Tacoma waterline. It's the only lighthouse in the area and was added in the 1930s. The first lighthouse was established there in 1903 and was a much less grand wooden structure with a kerosene lantern.

As far back as the 1840s, charts have referenced the area as Browns Point. It is uncertain, however, if the point was named after a member of the British expedition or from the 1870s US expedition that came through the area later. Some speculate that it was simply named Brown Point or Point Brown because it was rather brown.

In 1903, when the first lighthouse keeper, Oscar Brown, arrived, it was a miraculous coincidence that the point and the lightkeeper shared a name. Brown remained the lighthouse keeper for decades, even overseeing the upgrade to the Art Deco lighthouse. When the concrete lighthouse was built, it was equipped with an electric foghorn. The old fog bell that was used prior to that ended up being donated to the University of Puget Sound, where they used it to signal classes. By 1984, the bell was moved again, this time to Fox Island Alliance Church, where it remained until

2000. That July, the bell was finally returned to Browns Point, where the historical society installed it in the old pump house and rigged up a bowling ball to be used as the clapper.

Today the lighthouse has been remarkably restored, and the lightkeeper's cottage remains under the stewardship of the Points Northeast Historical Society. The Brown family stayed on as the lightkeepers at the lighthouse from 1903 until Oscar Brown retired in 1939, and the US Coast Guard took over maintenance and responsibility for the lighthouse.

Now that the Points Northeast Historical Society cares for the lighthouse keeper's cottage, anyone has a chance to go and stay. It's run as an Airbnb and has a lot of the cozy Pacific Northwest charm you'd hope for.

BLACKWELL MANSION

CITY'S FIRST LUXURY HOME

WHAT: A founding family's grand mansion

WHERE: 401 Broadway

COST: Prices vary for tours with Pretty Gritty Tours.

PRO TIP: If you don't want to wait for a tour of the building, you can always rent it. The top floor attic was converted into an Airbnb and is open for rentals. If you want to stay in one of Tacoma's finest mansions, this is your chance.

Why is Tacoma's first family little known in the city?

The Blackwells were one of Tacoma's most influential families. They hold the title for several of the city's firsts, and they were remarkable humanitarians. Despite their significance, their name is rarely seen on streets or buildings. Their anonymity seems to stem from their selfless acts during Tacoma's hardest times.

They were the first people to arrive in Tacoma by train and ran Tacoma's first hotel, the Blackwell. In 1891, they built Tacoma's most expensive home, hosting luminaries like Rudyard Kipling, Mark Twain, and North Pole explorers.

Photo courtesy of Tacoma Public Library

William Blackwell served as a territorial legislator, while Alice Blackwell established Tacoma's first orchard and garden, providing food and flowers to the city, including for its first funeral. They founded banks, libraries, community kitchens, and the Tacoma Humane Society. When the 1893 financial collapse struck, they sacrificed nearly everything, liquidating their institutions to feed the city. They kept only their 1891 mansion, which they opened as a refuge for those in need.

Their humanitarian efforts extended beyond grand gestures. When Alice's sister was widowed, the Blackwells adopted her two youngest children. One of them, Ruby, became a schoolteacher and authored a book about Tacoma's pioneering days. Her collection of traditional Puyallup baskets, now housed in the Washington State History Museum, remains one of the best preserved in the region.

The Blackwells also fought against the Chinese expulsion. Despite losing their wealth, they never lost their compassion. They died in their mansion in the 1920s, and Ruby ensured their legacy by donating their artifacts to the museum and selling the mansion to the YWCA to continue providing refuge. The Blackwells were icons of resilience, generosity, and the enduring essence of Tacoma. Today their 1891 mansion remains on Broadway as a testament to one of the city's finest families that no one seems to know.

As of today, it is a work rental space, but you can tour the former mansion and experience the majesty of one of Tacoma's most important families.

LEMAY CAR MUSEUM

How do you become America's car museum?

Affectionately known as America's Car Museum, the LeMay Car Museum isn't a secret, but the treasures inside can be. The collection of 1930s coach cars and automobiles is stunning. You can trace the arc of luxury cars through the British sports cars of the 1960s and the muscle cars that were used in rallies. The large 165,000-square-foot building looks reminiscent of an air intake on an American muscle car. The LeMay collection began south of Tacoma in a sprawling complex that served as a military school as well as a retirement community for nuns. The Marymount facility houses ephemera, Model Ts, and even a room dedicated to vintage radios. The hushed sound and the rich scent of history waft down quiet halls. The LeMay family has been collecting for generations now, and the Marymount collection is a stunning array of automobiles and more. The finest of that selection ended up at America's Car Museum in Tacoma.

COLLECTION OF VINTAGE CARS

WHAT: America's Car Museum

WHERE: 2702 E D St.

COST: Fee for admission

PRO TIP: Plan to visit both the LeMay Car Museum and the LeMay Collection at Marymount to compare and contrast.

Tacoma has some incredible museums, like the Washington State History Museum, Museum of Glass, Foss Waterway Seaport Museum, Tacoma Art Museum, Buffalo Soldiers Museum, and more.

At its peak, the LeMay collection had more than 3,000 automobiles and rooms upon rooms of enchanting artifacts. Many of those cars were sent to Tacoma where they make up the collection in the LeMay Car Museum.

Now this incredible museum sits in Tacoma and offers a chance for any car enthusiast to see some really cool cars. Not only that, though. They have a racing simulator, if you want to try your hand behind the wheel.

THE OLYMPUS

Was there an underground jazz club below Tacoma's hotel?

In the basement of the Hotel Olympus in Tacoma is a little-known part of history, now abandoned. In the basement was a bar that rebranded in 1944 as the Mirror Room. The Mirror Room was the center of Tacoma's jazz scene.

What gave the Olympus an edge was that it didn't refuse rooms or service to people of color. Before the Civil Rights Movement ended segregation, many hotels wouldn't allow people of color to stay there. The Hotel Olympus was open to all people, and it was across the street from USO #2, which

was the United Service Organization for service members of color. Hotel Olympus was the ideal location for several talented jazz musicians to perform in Tacoma.

When business got slow in the 1980s the decision was made to simply shutter the bar of grand marble and angled mirrors, sealing up a chapter of Tacoma's history below ground.

One part of this building's legacy that survived is the Mirror Room's iconic carved bar back. On the main floor of the Olympus building today is a restaurant called The Forum. This restaurant still has the large wooden bar with the carved likenesses of bearded men wearing hoods that support the dark oak shelves and stained glass that holds all the bottles. This bar was carved by French monks and was originally bound for California. The story goes that the bar was put up as stakes in a game of poker and lost to the Olympus, where it has remained ever since.

HIDDEN CLUB BELOW A RESTAURANT

WHAT: One of Tacoma's most important buildings, with an abandoned restaurant in the basement

WHERE: 815 Pacific Ave. A

COST: Depends on your dinner

PRO TIP: All of the mosaic tile in the Olympus and the restaurant, The Forum, is the original tile from the 1909 establishment.

Today you can see the four poker suits carved onto the side of the bar to remind everyone why it's here in Tacoma instead of California.

ALMOND ROCA

BELOVED TACOMA CANDYMAKER

WHAT: The original Almond Roca factory

WHERE: 110 E 26th St.

COST: Very affordable

PRO TIP: Try the variety box of Mountain Bars. They sell all three flavors—original, cherry, and peanut butter—in a 15-piece box. Then you can decide for yourself what the best flavor is. It's peanut butter, though.

What do Elvis, Tacoma, and chocolate all have in common?

One of the world's most famous candies is produced exclusively here in Tacoma. Off East 26th Street is a former shoe factory that dynamic duo Harry Brown and J. C. Haley purchased in 1919. The two of them had been in business together since 1912. Brown was a master chocolatier and confectioner. Haley was a shrewd businessman and philanthropist. Together, they created a candy company that has withstood the test of time.

Brown & Haley make a variety of chocolates and one of their signature items is the Mountain Bar. By far the most famous candy is Almond Roca, invented in 1923. It's a small log-shaped candy made of crunchy butter toffee, dipped in chocolate and rolled in crushed almonds. The local librarian gave it the name Almond Roca as an homage to the candy's Spanish-inspired origins.

Brown & Haley continue to operate. Their original factory still makes the candy that the world has come to know and love. As the slogan goes, "Brown & Haley make them daily." Today there is a small hut in the parking lot of the factory. The hut is actually a ticket booth from the 1962 Seattle World's Fair. Elvis used the ticket booth as his green room and trailer while in Seattle filming the movie *It Happened At the World's Fair*. Haley was a huge Elvis fan, and at the conclusion of the World's Fair he bought the ticket booth Elvis had used and brought it to Tacoma, where it has served as the retail location in town ever since.

Tacoma is also the town where Irv Robbins of Baskin-Robbins grew up in the ice cream business. His father owned and operated the Olympic Dairy.

OSCAR HEINRICH

Who was the American Sherlock Holmes?

Oscar Heinrich was a chemist who moved with his family to Tacoma in 1890 when he was 9 years old. He was the youngest of three children but assumed responsibility for his family when he was only 16 years old, after his father died by suicide in 1897. He trained to be a chemist and pharmacist and returned to Tacoma where he was employed as the city chemist.

The corruption in Tacoma was rampant in the early 1900s, and Heinrich had a difficult time using reason and science to move the city along. He resigned from his position at city hall and in 1910 began his own business. The Heinrich Technical Laboratory was on A Street. It would come to be known internationally as "the nation's first private crime lab." Heinrich grew increasingly interested in criminology and felt that he could offer more to the world of crime scene investigation.

THE BEGINNING OF POLICE FORENSICS

WHAT: America's Sherlock Holmes

WHERE: 3214 N 30th St. (Heinrich's former home) and 100 S 9th St. (Heinrich's former lab neighborhood)

COST: Free

PRO TIP: The Bowes Building, located at 100 S 9th St., was next door to Heinrich's first lab. It still has a very noir feeling to it. The Savage-Scofield Building, where Oscar's first lab was located, was demolished.

He had watched the police in Tacoma arrest and convict people with little to no evidence other than the stories they could collect from "sweating" confessions out of people.

With his scientific methods, Heinrich served as an expert witness in many of Tacoma's criminal cases, but perhaps the one that cemented his fame was the case of a woman found

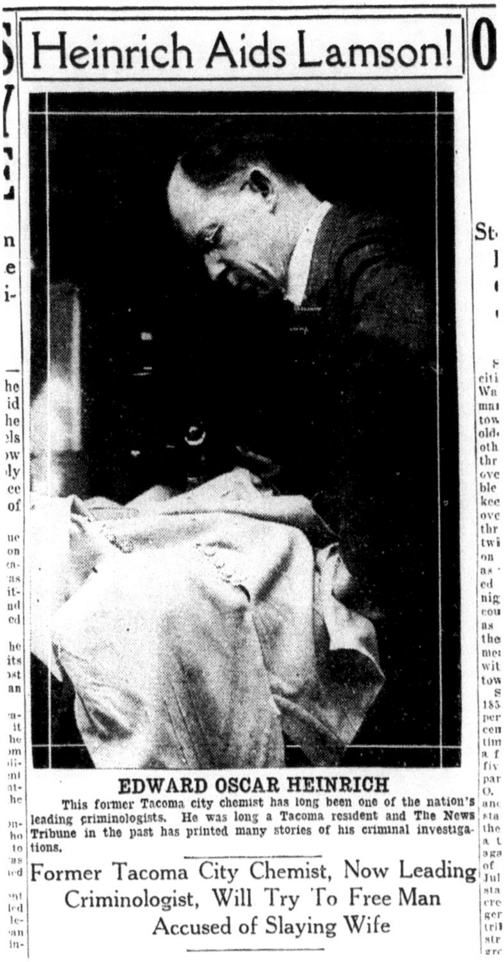

Heinrich Aids Lamson!

EDWARD OSCAR HEINRICH

This former Tacoma city chemist has long been one of the nation's leading criminologists. He was long a Tacoma resident and The News Tribune in the past has printed many stories of his criminal investigations.

Former Tacoma City Chemist, Now Leading Criminologist, Will Try To Free Man Accused of Slaying Wife

Photo courtesy of newspapers.com, Tacoma News Tribune

dead in her home with a revolver next to her. Oscar pioneered ballistic analysis, blood spatter study, and microscopic study of trace evidence. With his methods, documentation, and attention to detail, Heinrich helped to see the murdered woman's husband go to jail for staging her murder as a suicide.

Oscar Heinrich eventually left Tacoma and started teaching criminology and forensic crime scene analysis at Berkeley. When Heinrich died in 1953, he was widely applauded as America's Sherlock Holmes and the father of modern crime scene investigation.

The downtown corridor of Tacoma still has the feeling of a mystery novel. As you walk around, it is easy to imagine a 1930s detective working a case.

AROUND THE WORLD IN 80 DAYS

Did a Tacoma influencer inspire *Around the World in Eighty Days*?

George Francis Train was an eccentric millionaire who financed the Union Pacific Railroad and really loved Tacoma. Originally from Boston, he spent much of his life on the road and much of his time promoting his holdings and business interests in Tacoma. Locally, he was lovingly referred to as "The Psycho." When he would come to Tacoma it was with a ferocious energy. He would spend all his time visiting people in town and throwing big events to promote the city.

Train was known for many things, but it was his global travels that made him famous. In 1870, he took off and circumnavigated the globe. He spent 80 days in total traveling (with a quick two-month stint in a French prison because he was supporting the Paris Commune). After his friend and noted author Alexandre Dumas helped the US government get Train out of prison, it is rumored that Jules Verne wrote his novel *Around the World in Eighty Days* about Train's fantastic voyage.

In 1890, American journalist Nellie Bly broke Train's 80-day record by making it around the world in 72 days. Train wouldn't let that stand, so he mounted a new expedition to

LAUNCH POINT FOR WORLD RECORD

WHAT: The spot where one of the first influencers set a record for going around the world

WHERE: 926 Broadway

COST: Free

PRO TIP: While Train did mention the Tacoma Aroma, it was never clarified what he meant.

Photo courtesy of Library of Congress

circumnavigate the world, and this time he used his favorite city, Tacoma, as the launch point. Train promoted Tacoma as the finest and most modern city on the West Coast. He famously wrote, "Seattle! Seattle! Death Rattle, Death Rattle; Tacoma! Tacoma! Aroma, Aroma! Now is Tacoma's time!" Train is also one of the many to receive credit for giving Tacoma the moniker of "The City of Destiny."

George Train left Tacoma on March 18, 1890, and returned 67 days, 12 hours, and one minute later, setting a new record.

Modoc's Market is in the Wabash Downtown Historic District, recognized by the National Register of Historic Places and the Historic Landmarks Foundation of Indiana.

Hosmer House

SOURCES

Goddess of Commerce
Tacoma News Tribune, January 2004

Gray Ships
navsource.org/archives/09/54/540010.htm

Hidden Bathhouse
lmtribune.com/northwest/bathhouse-with-seedy-past-rediscovered-under-tacoma-f7260426

Fawcett's Faucet
metroparkstacoma.org

The Spanish Cannon in Wright Park
newspapers.com/image/737677707/?match=1&terms=spanish%20cannon%2C%20wright%20park

The Nymphs
parkstacoma.gov/wp-content/uploads/2019/05/WrightPark_Master-Plan-Report.pdf

Tacoma's Tunnel Network
groupssa.com/ssa/tacomatunnel.html

The Birthplace of Noir
tacomahistory.live/2020/03/07/the-game-is-afoot-watson

A Bank Vault You Can Hang Out In
seattletimes.com/business/real-estate/1920s-tacoma-tower-with-bank-vault-to-be-renovated-for-housing

The Seymour Botanical Conservatory
metroparkstacoma.org/place/wright-park

The World's Tallest and Longest Bicycle Bridge
newspapers.com/image/736227544/?match=1&terms=bicycle%20bridge

The Whistling Well
newspapers.com/image/724606991/?match=1&terms=whistling%20well%20

St. Luke's Moving Church
stlukestacoma.org

The Chihuly Bridge of Glass
azahner.com/works/chihuly-bridge

Tacoma's Liberty Bell
tomlovesthelibertybell.com/washington-liberty-bell-replica

Old St. Peters
oldstpeters.org

Old City Hall's Jail Cells
oldcityhalltacoma.com

Sub-Sidewalk Bathroom
tacomahistory.live

Tacoma's Moving Sidewalks
cdm17061.contentdm.oclc.org/digital/collection/p17061coll21/id/4772/rec/4

Ivan's Face Prints
historylink.org/file/20534

Bob's Java Jive
southsoundmag.com/eat-drink/the-legendary-history-of-bob-s-java-jive-lives-up-to-rumor-mill/article_baf19c28-22d7-51e8-9869-e9d9926b3114.html

Earthquake Statue
newspapers.com/image/741746446/?match=1&terms=Kelcy%20allen%20

Foss Seaport
fosswaterwayseaport.org

Hidden Mural
newspapers.com/image/741615312/?match=1&terms=Mary%20Mann%2C%20mural

Chutes and Ladders
parkstacoma.gov/place/dune-peninsula

Trashasaurus Rex
reddit.com/r/Tacoma/comments/177bp4f/a_scrap_art_trex_once_dreamed_of_having_normal

The Brewery Lamp Post
National Register of Historic Places inventory—nomination form—Pacific Brewing and Malting Company

Tacoma's Missing Chinatown
tacomamethod.com/aftermath

An Old Scientific Zoo on the Roof
newspapers.com/image/725358125/?terms=scientific%20zoo%20

Zanetta and the Turnip
"Can Zanetta Catch Turnip from Top of Realty Building," *Tacoma Daily Ledger*, April 19, 1912

Telephone Museum
nashgroupcpas.com/tacoma-telephone-pioneer-museum

Post Office Peepholes
rutherfordtnhistory.org/hidden-spy-system-still-exists-in-the-old-post-office

Blue Mouse
bluemousetheatre.com/history

Bear Pit
cdm17061.contentdm.oclc.org/digital/collection/p17061coll21/id/7299/rec/2

Railroad HQ
washingtonhistory.org/exhibit/northern-pacific-tacoma

Top of the Ocean
historylink.org/File/9818

Tacoma Dome
tacomadome.org/dome-info/venue-story

Freighthouse Square
visitpiercecounty.com/listing/freighthouse-square/96

Armory
historylink.org/file/10452

Tacoma's Streetcar Disaster
historylink.org/file/7477

Pauper's Field Cemetery
tacomalibrary.org/blogs/post/paupers-field

Tacoma Narrows
wsdot.wa.gov/tnbhistory/bridges-aftermath.htm

Tacoma's Sea Monster
"An Electric Monster," *Tacoma Daily Ledger*, July 3, 1893

Horse Track Center
groupssa.com/ssa/tacomahorsetracks.html

Monkeyshines
gritcitymag.com/2020/01/a-little-backstory-on-monkeyshines-in-tacoma

Haunted Bradley
tacomapub.com/about/index.html

Tacoma's Missing Totem Pole
cityoftacoma.org/UserFiles/Servers/Server_6/File/cms/cedd/TacomaCulture/Arts/TA_PublicArt_TotemPoleDeaccessionOverview.pdf

Missing Safe
Interview with Robert Mester, May 12, 2019, and January 28, 2021

Charlotte's Free Blueberry Park
parkstacoma.gov/place/charlottes-blueberry-park

Never Never Land Statues
Interview with general manger Jim Reuter, September 7, 2024

The Mountaineer Tree
naturalatlas.com/plants/trees/mountaineer-2152259

Herbert Dune Park
parkstacoma.gov/place/dune-peninsula

UFOs in Tacoma
seattlesouthside.com/things-to-do/sightseeing/seattle-southside-scenes/art/maury-island-ufo-incident-mural

Chambers Bay Tunnels
chambersbaygolf.com/history

Stadium High School
stadium.tacomaschools.org/about/stadiums-history

Rust Mansion
historylink.org/File/20737

Hosmer House
southsoundtalk.com/2018/10/03/hosmer-house-the-oldest-residence-in-downtown-tacoma

Buffalo Soldiers Museum
army.mil/article/224264/woman_fights_to_save_memory_of_historic_soldiers_near_joint_base_lewis_mcchord

The Proctor Clock
tacomaweekly.com/proctor-clock-getting-some-tlc-p4888-117.htm

Jack the Bear
thenewstribune.com/news/local/article25881052.html

Mason's Mummy
theolympian.com/living/article25281733.html

Rebecca Carr
jobcarrmuseum.org/blog/tacoma-s-founding-mothers-rebecca-vail-pitman-carr-staley

Snake Lake Paradise
metroparkstacoma.org/a-young-environmental-movement-rose-up-50-years-ago-to-save-tacomas-snake-lake

Point Defiance
metroparkstacoma.org/point-defiance-park-history

Salishan's Forgotten City
mynorthwest.com/history/explore-layers-of-history-at-tacomas-swan-creek-park/3453028

Puget Gulch Park
parkstacoma.gov/place/puget-park

Haddaway Hall
olmstedonline.org/RelatedDocument/WebLink/61

Elks Temple
southsoundmag.com/arts-entertainment/the-rich-history-of-mcmenamins-elks-temple/article_1252aedb-9b01-5f2b-8ee7-5264a9a18e7b.html

Frisko Freeze
cms.cityoftacoma.org/planning/historic-preservation/NominationDocs/1201%20Division%20Ave,%20Frisko%20Freeze.pdf

Prairie Line Trail
prairielinetrail.org

The Last Stone Owl
thenewstribune.com/news/local/article62012317.html

O'Neil Cast Iron Museum
lodgecastiron.com/story/marg-larry-oneil-welcome-biggest-cast-iron-collection-planet?srsltid=AfmBOopvVgzPkawm-jf3SPMCXqlQ2ajiFbsKQKd29MT8zeAxCLZCs4p8

The Elephant House
washingtonhistory.org/wp-content/uploads/2021/01/32-3-Fall-2018-CM_wCover_lo-rez.pdf

The Changer
southsoundtalk.com/2023/12/22/buried-stone-of-the-changer-will-likely-remain-a-mystery-in-tacoma

Andelana
historylink.org/File/20949

Old Woman's Gulch
Tacoma, Its History and Its Builders by Herbert Hunt

Engine House No. 9
southsoundtalk.com/2016/03/17/engine-house-no-9-tacoma

Browns Point Lighthouse
pointsnortheast.org

Blackwell Mansion
Tacoma, Its History and Its Builders by Herbert Hunt

LeMay Car Museum
americascarmuseum.org/?gad_source=1&gclid=CjwKCAiAkc28BhB0EiwAM001TbDMzB4o6KRxGvyGBR_h3V0fRBeDkLbfcnwE8geEgUB_Jfi6itgX2RoCFb8QAvD_BwE

The Olympus
tacomahistory.live/2018/03/31/in-the-shadow/#:~:text=The%20Olympus%20Hotel%20was%20designed,Stradivarius%20than%20a%20second%20fiddle

Almond Roca
brown-haley.com/about-us

Oscar Heinrich
American Sherlock by Kate Dawson

Around the World in 80 Days
cascadepbs.org/mossback/2024/11/mossbacks-northwest-1800s-influencer-obsessed-tacoma

Union Station

INDEX

Lady Washington at the Foss Seaport

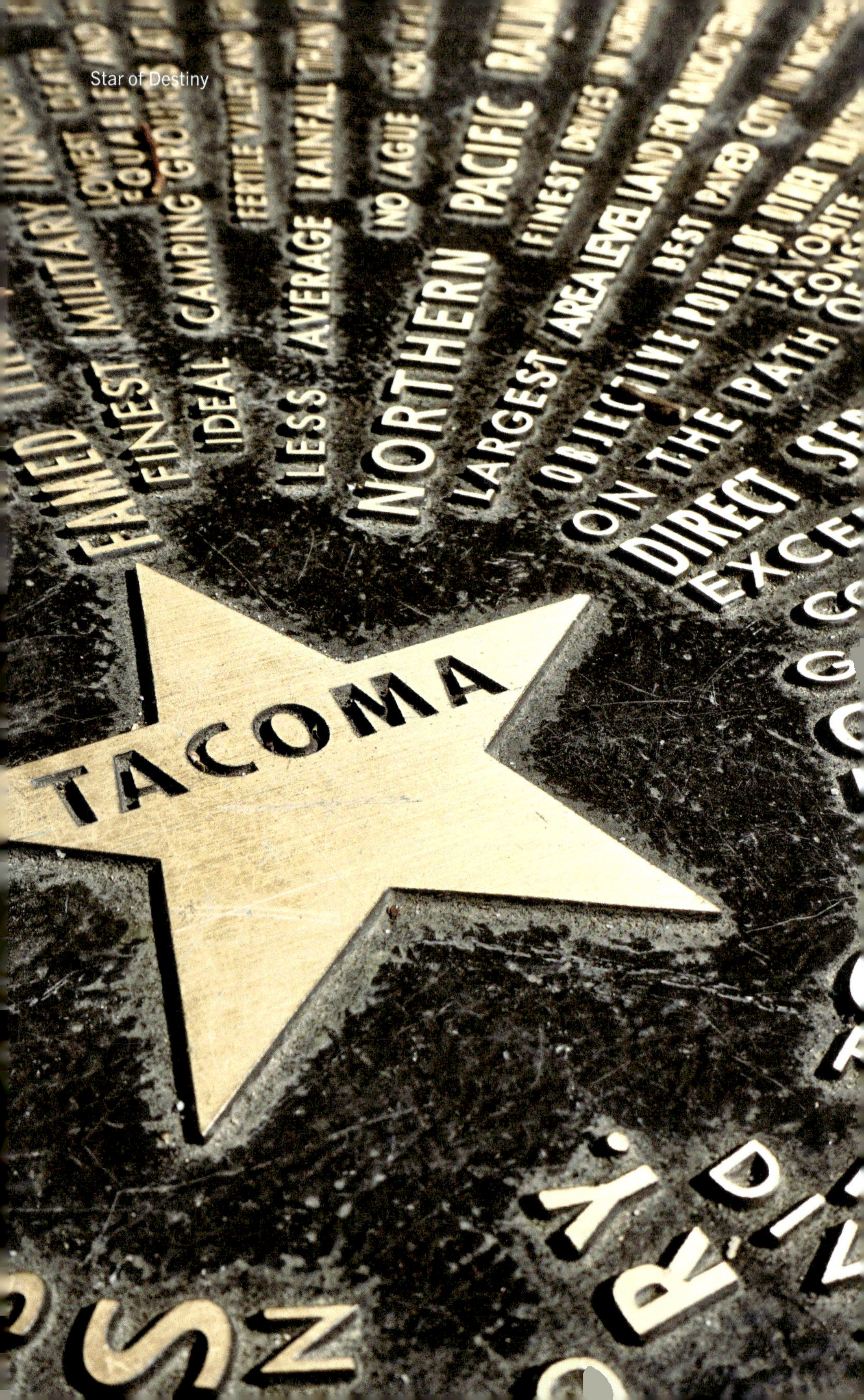

Star of Destiny